# MORE JUMBLE CROSSWORDS

# Jumble + Crosswords = Ultimate Brain-Bender Fun

## by David L. Hoyt

TRIUMPH
B O O K S
CHICAGO

This book is available at special discounts
for your group or organization.

For further information, contact:

Triumph Books
601 South LaSalle Street
Suite 500
Chicago, Illinois 60605
(312) 939-3330
(312) 663-3557 FAX

ISBN 1-57243-386-8

Printed in the USA

This book is available in quantity at special discounts for your group or organization.

For further information, contact:
Triumph Books
814 North Franklin Street
Chicago, Illinois 60610


ISBN 978-1-57243-386-1

Printed in the United States of America

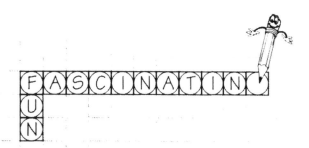

FUN FASCINATING

# MORE JUMBLE CROSSWORDS

## CONTENTS

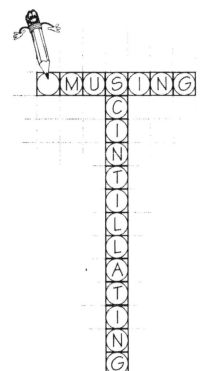

MUSING SCINTILLATING

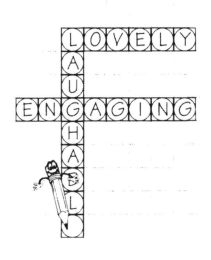

LOVELY LAUGHABLE ENGAGING

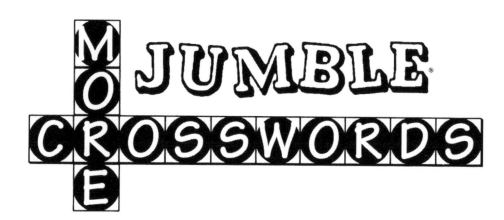

# MORE JUMBLE® CROSSWORDS

## CHAMPION PUZZLES

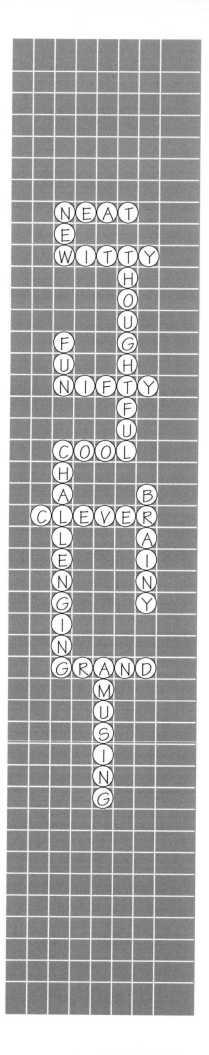

# JUMBLE CROSSWORDS™

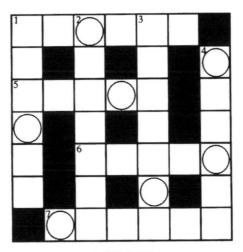

## ACROSS

| CLUE | ANSWER |
|---|---|
| 1. An indication of trouble | A T T E R H |
| 5. A platform | T R A A L |
| 6. Greased | B U L D E |
| 7. *Paperback* _____ | T I R W R E |

## DOWN

| CLUE | ANSWER |
|---|---|
| 1. _____ out | D A T H W E |
| 2. Known for its sound | T T R R A L E |
| 3. A perfomer | C A R T A B O |
| 4. Nicer | D R E N I K |

**CLUE:** Difficult to deal with

**BONUS**

How to play — Complete the crossword puzzle by looking at the clues and unscrambling the answers. When the puzzle is complete, unscramble the circled letters to solve the BONUS.

# JUMBLE CROSSWORDS™

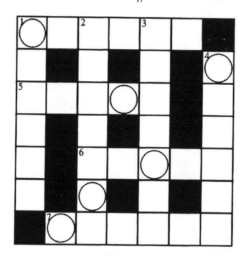

## ACROSS

| CLUE | ANSWER |
|---|---|
| 1. One of seven | CAAIRF |
| 5. A man's name | GLENI |
| 6. _____ circle or ear | RENNI |
| 7. *Snipes* first name | SLEWYE |

## DOWN

| CLUE | ANSWER |
|---|---|
| 1. Known as the "Terminator" | DONRAL |
| 2. A type of music | EITARMG |
| 3. A rank | CLENOOL |
| 4. Not far away | BRANYE |

**CLUE:** Wayne Knight plays this character

# BONUS ◯◯◯◯◯◯

How to play — Complete the crossword puzzle by looking at the clues and unscrambling the answers. When the puzzle is complete, unscramble the circled letters to solve the BONUS.

# JUMBLE CROSSWORDS™

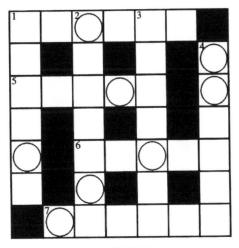

### ACROSS

| CLUE | ANSWER |
|------|--------|
| 1. *The National _____* | MENTAH |
| 5. Worn out, exhausted | TSNPE |
| 6. Cause to laugh | MUAES |
| 7. Around the longest | TOSLED |

### DOWN

| CLUE | ANSWER |
|------|--------|
| 1. Aid | SSSIAT |
| 2. Part of a foot | OLTINAE |
| 3. Excite | STNEEHU |
| 4. Closest to the bottom | TLWOSE |

**CLUE:** You are working on one now

BONUS ◯◯◯◯◯◯◯◯

How to play  Complete the crossword puzzle by looking at the clues and unscrambling the answers. When the puzzle is complete, unscramble the circled letters to solve the BONUS.

4

# JUMBLE CROSSWORDS™

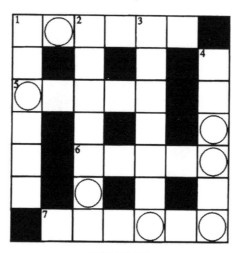

## ACROSS

| CLUE | ANSWER |
|------|--------|
| 1. Keep quiet | F Y C I A P |
| 5. You can *take* these | S T O E N |
| 6. Toughen through use | I R N U E |
| 7. Inferior or cheap | H E C E Y S |

## DOWN

| CLUE | ANSWER |
|------|--------|
| 1. Penalize | S I P N U H |
| 2. Found in water | S C A F I T H |
| 3. A groove | E F R I S U S |
| 4. Probable | L E L K I Y |

**CLUE:** Long associated with a man named George

BONUS

How to play    Complete the crossword puzzle by looking at the clues and unscrambling the answers. When the puzzle is complete, unscramble the circled letters to solve the BONUS.

5

# PUZZLE #5

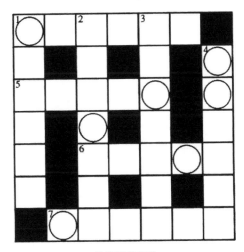

## JUMBLE CROSSWORDS™

### ACROSS

| CLUE | ANSWER |
|------|--------|
| 1. Very little rhymes with this | GANERO |
| 5. A saying | DAAEG |
| 6. This is a crime | SNORA |
| 7. Dull | DYSTOG |

### DOWN

| CLUE | ANSWER |
|------|--------|
| 1. A shrine | CARLEO |
| 2. Unyielding | MADNAAT |
| 3. Supposed | SEESDUG |
| 4. An animal sound | YIHNWN |

**CLUE:** Not specified

## BONUS ◯◯◯◯◯◯◯

How to play — Complete the crossword puzzle by looking at the clues and unscrambling the answers. When the puzzle is complete, unscramble the circled letters to solve the BONUS.

# #6

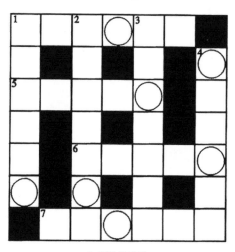

## JUMBLE CROSSWORDS™

**ACROSS**

| CLUE | ANSWER |
|------|--------|
| 1. Easily moved | LOBIME |
| 5. Sane | ILDCU |
| 6. To move upward | BIMCL |
| 7. A small hound | AELGEB |

**DOWN**

| CLUE | ANSWER |
|------|--------|
| 1. Free from tension | WELOML |
| 2. This has two wheels | LCYICBE |
| 3. Housing | NLGOGID |
| 4. Agile | BENMIL |

**CLUE:** There was one in 'Beetlejuice', and another in 'Sliver'

**BONUS** ◯◯◯◯◯◯◯

How to play — Complete the crossword puzzle by looking at the clues and unscrambling the answers. When the puzzle is complete, unscramble the circled letters to solve the BONUS.

# JUMBLE CROSSWORDS™

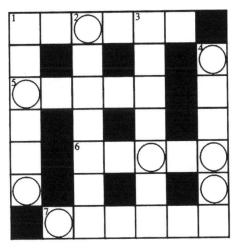

### ACROSS

| CLUE | ANSWER |
|------|--------|
| 1. A religious leader | H A D U B D |
| 5. *Billy Ray's* last name | R S C Y U |
| 6. A *belt* color | L K C A B |
| 7. Least | W E S T E F |

### DOWN

| CLUE | ANSWER |
|------|--------|
| 1. Grow to be | E M C O E B |
| 2. Long lasting | B A R E D L U |
| 3. A type of *situation* | H A T S O E G |
| 4. A container | B T E U K C |

**CLUE:** Yours is welcomed

**BONUS**

How to play  Complete the crossword puzzle by looking at the clues and unscrambling the answers. When the puzzle is complete, unscramble the circled letters to solve the BONUS.

8

# #8

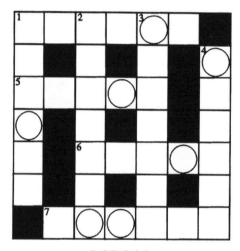

## JUMBLE CROSSWORDS™

### ACROSS

| CLUE | | ANSWER |
|------|--|--------|
| 1. | A maladjusted person | STIMFI |
| 5. | Bought in pairs | HESSO |
| 6. | An award | LMAED |
| 7. | Woman's first name | DIGNIR |

### DOWN

| CLUE | | ANSWER |
|------|--|--------|
| 1. | Gather | TUMRES |
| 2. | Performer | SNAHMOW |
| 3. | Someone in the know | DINISRE |
| 4. | Covered | LEVEDI |

**CLUE:** Classic

**BONUS**

How to play  Complete the crossword puzzle by looking at the clues and unscrambling the answers. When the puzzle is complete, unscramble the circled letters to solve the BONUS.

# PUZZLE

# #9

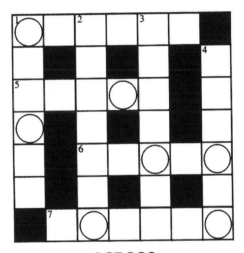

## JUMBLE CROSSWORDS™

### ACROSS

| CLUE | ANSWER |
| --- | --- |
| 1. Away from the coast | NNIALD |
| 5. A negative | SNIMU |
| 6. Third of nine | TRAHE |
| 7. Used for emphasis | CTIILA |

### DOWN

| CLUE | ANSWER |
| --- | --- |
| 1. A confined person | TAMINE |
| 2. Tolerant | TENLENI |
| 3. Air passes through this | NLOISTR |
| 4. A style of architecture | CGTOIH |

**CLUE:** A reason to take a seat

## BONUS

**How to play** Complete the crossword puzzle by looking at the clues and unscrambling the answers. When the puzzle is complete, unscramble the circled letters to solve the BONUS.

10

# JUMBLE CROSSWORDS™

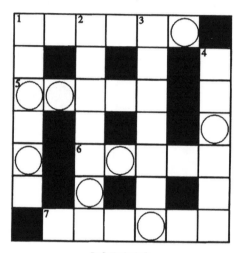

### ACROSS

| CLUE | ANSWER |
|------|--------|
| 1. Take for granted | S M S E U A |
| 5. Flat, level | N L E A P |
| 6. A type of comparison | T A R O I |
| 7. Dives | S P W O S O |

### DOWN

| CLUE | ANSWER |
|------|--------|
| 1. Like a large mountain | P I A L E N |
| 2. This can fly | W O R R A S P |
| 3. A master | M O A R E T S |
| 4. Composed of veins | O V N E S U |

**CLUE:** Born in 1769, died in 1821

BONUS

How to play — Complete the crossword puzzle by looking at the clues and unscrambling the answers. When the puzzle is complete, unscramble the circled letters to solve the BONUS.

# JUMBLE CROSSWORDS™

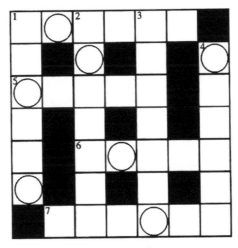

### ACROSS

| CLUE | ANSWER |
|------|--------|
| 1. "Star Trek's" *DeForest* | Y K L L E E |
| 5. Hurled | N S U L G |
| 6. Rub together | N R D I G |
| 7. A *cracker* | R G H A M A |

### DOWN

| CLUE | ANSWER |
|------|--------|
| 1. These go with *hugs* | S K S S E I |
| 2. Furniture nickname | L R E G U O N |
| 3. *Muffin* descriptor | G E H S L I N |
| 4. Intelligence | O I M S D W |

**CLUE:** Gives abundantly

## BONUS

**How to play** Complete the crossword puzzle by looking at the clues and unscrambling the answers. When the puzzle is complete, unscramble the circled letters to solve the BONUS.

# #12

## JUMBLE CROSSWORDS™

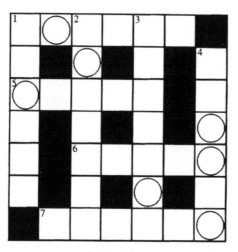

### ACROSS

| CLUE | ANSWER |
|------|--------|
| 1. Found on a bed or sofa | WPLIOL |
| 5. *Edouard's* last name | TAMEN |
| 6. Correct | EEDMN |
| 7. Taken | ENLOST |

### DOWN

| CLUE | ANSWER |
|------|--------|
| 1. *Anderson's* first name | LAMEAP |
| 2. "The _____ Yard" | TSOLGEN |
| 3. Served in a bowl | MTLAEOA |
| 4. Not in view | DHEIND |

**CLUE:** A singer, field or rock

**BONUS** ◯◯◯◯◯◯◯

How to play — Complete the crossword puzzle by looking at the clues and unscrambling the answers. When the puzzle is complete, unscramble the circled letters to solve the BONUS.

# P U Z Z L E

## #13

## JUMBLE CROSSWORDS™

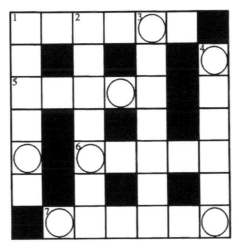

### ACROSS

| CLUE | ANSWER |
|---|---|
| 1. From a northern U.S. state | E Y N A K E |
| 5. A car manufacturer | S T O L U |
| 6. Wash | S N R I E |
| 7. Tired | E Y P E L S |

### DOWN

| CLUE | ANSWER |
|---|---|
| 1. A color | Y W L E O L |
| 2. To be expected | T A N L A R U |
| 3. Substance | S N E E C S E |
| 4. A "King" novel and movie | M R E Y S I |

**CLUE:** This person plays a doctor on TV

## BONUS

**How to play**  Complete the crossword puzzle by looking at the clues and unscrambling the answers. When the puzzle is complete, unscramble the circled letters to solve the BONUS.

14

# JUMBLE CROSSWORDS™

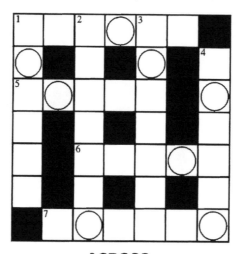

## ACROSS

| CLUE | ANSWER |
|------|--------|
| 1. "Kidman's" first name | C L O E I N |
| 5. A woman's name | B L A E M |
| 6. Gets closer | S N R E A |
| 7. Did not leave | S D Y A T E |

## DOWN

| CLUE | ANSWER |
|------|--------|
| 1. A cloud | M U N S B I |
| 2. A counsel | T I N B A C E |
| 3. This can be sung | L B L U A Y L |
| 4. New | D U N S U E |

**CLUE:** Length, but not in inches or feet

**BONUS**

How to play — Complete the crossword puzzle by looking at the clues and unscrambling the answers. When the puzzle is complete, unscramble the circled letters to solve the BONUS.

# #15

## JUMBLE CROSSWORDS™

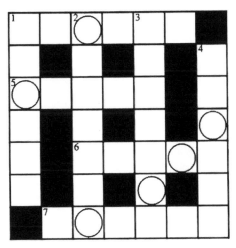

### ACROSS

| CLUE | ANSWER |
|------|--------|
| 1. Continue | SMEERU |
| 5. A "Key" | GROLA |
| 6. She stars in her own show | NEELL |
| 7. Result of bleaching | HITREW |

### DOWN

| CLUE | ANSWER |
|------|--------|
| 1. Remember | VRLEIE |
| 2. A sound | SHCEREC |
| 3. A _____ evening | TIMNOLO |
| 4. "Kathleen's" last name | NUTRRE |

**CLUE:** Enjoy

## BONUS

**How to play** Complete the crossword puzzle by looking at the clues and unscrambling the answers. When the puzzle is complete, unscramble the circled letters to solve the BONUS.

# JUMBLE CROSSWORDS™

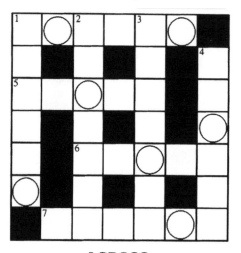

## ACROSS

| CLUE | ANSWER |
|------|--------|
| 1. Writer | C B E I R S |
| 5. Part of a garment | P L A E L |
| 6. A coating | G I N I C |
| 7. A famous "Mr." | N A P T U E |

## DOWN

| CLUE | ANSWER |
|------|--------|
| 1. Part of this must be rigid | N I L T S P |
| 2. A turtle is one | I R E E L T P |
| 3. One followed by nine zeros | L I B N I L O |
| 4. A goal | G R E A T T |

**CLUE:** Imagine

**BONUS**

How to play — Complete the crossword puzzle by looking at the clues and unscrambling the answers. When the puzzle is complete, unscramble the circled letters to solve the BONUS.

# JUMBLE CROSSWORDS™

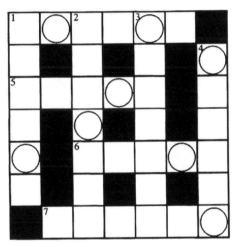

## ACROSS

| CLUE | ANSWER |
|---|---|
| 1. A sound | RULEGG |
| 5. Pale reddish purple | CLILA |
| 6. This is sun-dried | BEDAO |
| 7. Carefully chosen | SLEETC |

## DOWN

| CLUE | ANSWER |
|---|---|
| 1. Solar system's home | XALYGA |
| 2. This *form* is usually signed | SEELERA |
| 3. Found in milk | STALCEO |
| 4. Truthful | SHENTO |

CLUE: The *"H"* in *H.H., C.H., S.H., D.H., T.H., V.H.,* and *R.H*

BONUS

How to play   Complete the crossword puzzle by looking at the clues and unscrambling the answers. When the puzzle is complete, unscramble the circled letters to solve the BONUS.

18

# PUZZLE #18

JUMBLE CROSSWORDS™

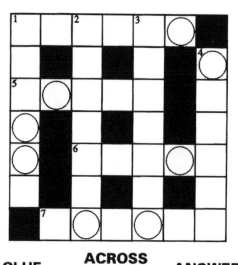

## ACROSS

| CLUE | ANSWER |
|------|--------|
| 1. Tempt | T E I C N E |
| 5. Raise | T S H I O |
| 6. Lacking sense | N N I A E |
| 7. Snow _____ | S K A L F E |

## DOWN

| CLUE | ANSWER |
|------|--------|
| 1. Admonish urgently | T X E R O H |
| 2. Of little importance | T L V I I A R |
| 3. This is often narrow | C T A A W K L |
| 4. Fixate | S B E O S S |

**CLUE:** Spectator

BONUS

How to play   Complete the crossword puzzle by looking at the clues and unscrambling the answers. When the puzzle is complete, unscramble the circled letters to solve the BONUS.

**#19**

# JUMBLE CROSSWORDS™

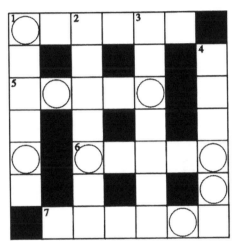

### ACROSS

| CLUE | ANSWER |
|------|--------|
| 1. A spider is one | TISCEN |
| 5. Singer *Abdul* | LAPUA |
| 6. Cartoon character's name | MERLE |
| 7. Full of turmoil | MYTSRO |

### DOWN

| CLUE | ANSWER |
|------|--------|
| 1. Bring in | TRIPOM |
| 2. Found in a classroom | SEDTTNU |
| 3. Sweet talker | RACHEMR |
| 4. Mechanical _____ | GRENYE |

**CLUE:** This often begins with a ceremony

**BONUS**

**How to play** Complete the crossword puzzle by looking at the clues and unscrambling the answers. When the puzzle is complete, unscramble the circled letters to solve the BONUS.

20

# #20

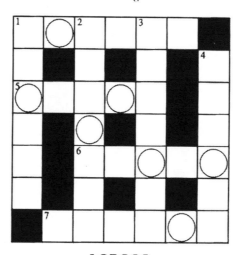

# JUMBLE CROSSWORDS™

## ACROSS

| CLUE | | ANSWER |
|------|---|--------|
| 1. | Dump | DALUNO |
| 5. | A man's name | EDNIW |
| 6. | Underdog's victory | STEPU |
| 7. | Found in Canada | TOTWAA |

## DOWN

| CLUE | | ANSWER |
|------|---|--------|
| 1. | Slanted to one side | VENUNE |
| 2. | This can be *filed* | SWITULA |
| 3. | A reason to be forgetful | SNAMEAI |
| 4. | Mystery writer's first name | HATAAG |

**CLUE:** A Harrison Ford movie

## BONUS

How to play    Complete the crossword puzzle by looking at the clues and unscrambling the answers. When the puzzle is complete, unscramble the circled letters to solve the BONUS.

 #21

# JUMBLE CROSSWORDS™

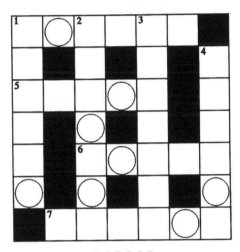

## ACROSS

| CLUE | ANSWER |
|------|--------|
| 1. Worn by most dogs | CLRAOL |
| 5. To decline markedly | SPLMU |
| 6. A "Day" | DIRSO |
| 7. Of inferior quality | STYRAH |

## DOWN

| CLUE | ANSWER |
|------|--------|
| 1. This grows on a tree | CHEASW |
| 2. To clean "dirty money" | DRANLUE |
| 3. Longs, aims, seeks | SPARSIE |
| 4. Messy place nickname | GSTIPY |

**CLUE:** You may be in yours now

BONUS

How to play — Complete the crossword puzzle by looking at the clues and unscrambling the answers. When the puzzle is complete, unscramble the circled letters to solve the BONUS.

# #22

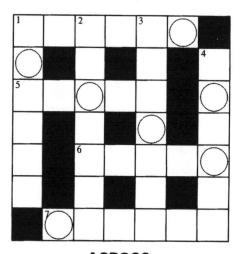

## JUMBLE CROSSWORDS™

### ACROSS

| CLUE | ANSWER |
|------|--------|
| 1. Out of shape | BLAYFB |
| 5. A car or house document | LETTI |
| 6. _____ on | DAKCE |
| 7. A cell | RUNEON |

### DOWN

| CLUE | ANSWER |
|------|--------|
| 1. Dad | TERHAF |
| 2. An individual item | AELRCTI |
| 3. A _____ box | REEKRBA |
| 4. The "J" in M.J. | RONADJ |

**CLUE:** Associated with "500"

## BONUS

How to play    Complete the crossword puzzle by looking at the clues and unscrambling the answers. When the puzzle is complete, unscramble the circled letters to solve the BONUS.

# JUMBLE CROSSWORDS™

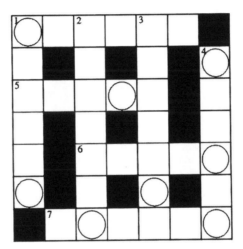

## ACROSS

| CLUE | ANSWER |
|------|--------|
| 1. *In* _____ | STIRED |
| 5. A recess in a wall | CINEH |
| 6. Taunt | ETSEA |
| 7. This has wings | RIGLED |

## DOWN

| CLUE | ANSWER |
|------|--------|
| 1. You can *lose* yours | NAYTIS |
| 2. A performance | CERLATI |
| 3. Person who resists change | HIDRADE |
| 4. Profession | ECRAER |

**CLUE:** One of a famous "threesome"

**BONUS**

How to play   Complete the crossword puzzle by looking at the clues and unscrambling the answers. When the puzzle is complete, unscramble the circled letters to solve the BONUS.

# JUMBLE CROSSWORDS™

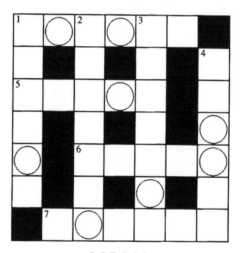

## ACROSS

| CLUE | | ANSWER |
|---|---|---|
| 1. | Dealt a blow | SKTCUR |
| 5. | Played by Michael York | GALON |
| 6. | _____ cannon | SLOEO |
| 7. | Attractive | TYPTER |

## DOWN

| CLUE | | ANSWER |
|---|---|---|
| 1. | A Tom Hanks movie | LPSHAS |
| 2. | Usual | GARELRU |
| 3. | To associate | CROTSNO |
| 4. | Happy | HYEREC |

**CLUE:** Sometimes marked with an "X"

**BONUS**

How to play — Complete the crossword puzzle by looking at the clues and unscrambling the answers. When the puzzle is complete, unscramble the circled letters to solve the BONUS.

# PUZZLE

 #25

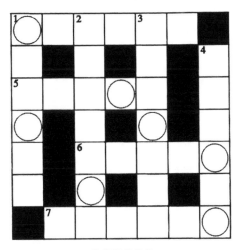

## JUMBLE CROSSWORDS™

### ACROSS

| CLUE | | ANSWER |
|------|--|--------|
| 1. | Sometimes served "frozen" | TOYGUR |
| 5. | Julia _____-Dreyfus | SLIUO |
| 6. | A flying machine | MBPIL |
| 7. | Bushes | SHDGEE |

### DOWN

| CLUE | | ANSWER |
|------|--|--------|
| 1. | "Big Bird's" color | LWYLEO |
| 2. | Complain | BURGMEL |
| 3. | Moving quickly | SHURGIN |
| 4. | Grounds, buildings | SPAMCU |

**CLUE:** This character's last name was 'Lindstrom'

## BONUS

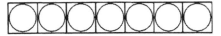

How to play    Complete the crossword puzzle by looking at the clues and unscrambling the answers. When the puzzle is complete, unscramble the circled letters to solve the BONUS.

26

# JUMBLE CROSSWORDS™

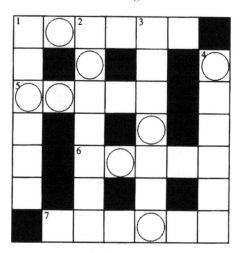

## ACROSS

| CLUE | ANSWER |
|------|--------|
| 1. Next to | S D B I E E |
| 5. Specialty | T R E O F |
| 6. Wanderer | D A N M O |
| 7. 'Frank' and 'Estelle's' son | O E G R E G |

## DOWN

| CLUE | ANSWER |
|------|--------|
| 1. Confuse | F L A B F E |
| 2. A golfing *Curtis* | R A T S G E N |
| 3. Someone with big plans | R E R E M A D |
| 4. A style of walking | L E D A D W |

**CLUE:** Shoes

BONUS

How to play  Complete the crossword puzzle by looking at the clues and unscrambling the answers. When the puzzle is complete, unscramble the circled letters to solve the BONUS.

27

# JUMBLE CROSSWORDS™

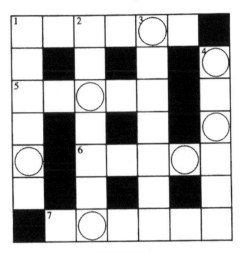

## ACROSS

| CLUE | | ANSWER |
|------|--|--------|
| 1. A *bewitching* "Dr." | | M O Y A B B |
| 5. A monetary unit | | P E R E U |
| 6. "Gloria's" mother | | T I D H E |
| 7. Bermuda or Puerto Rico | | D I N S A L |

## DOWN

| CLUE | | ANSWER |
|------|--|--------|
| 1. This can be *crossed* | | R E D R O B |
| 2. One is a famous frog | | M S P E P U T |
| 3. *North* or *South* _____ | | C R I M E A A |
| 4. _____ *out* in anger | | H L D E S A |

**CLUE:** Bread, milk, etc.

**BONUS**

**How to play** Complete the crossword puzzle by looking at the clues and unscrambling the answers. When the puzzle is complete, unscramble the circled letters to solve the BONUS.

# JUMBLE CROSSWORDS™

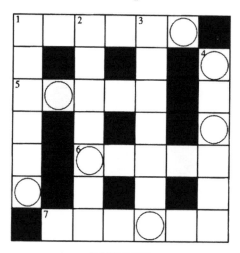

## ACROSS

| CLUE | ANSWER |
|------|--------|
| 1. A man or boy | EWLOLF |
| 5. The first extra inning | HTTNE |
| 6. She has her own show | NEELL |
| 7. Anger | GEAREN |

## DOWN

| CLUE | ANSWER |
|------|--------|
| 1. One equals six feet | MHAFOT |
| 2. This is portable | NATRELN |
| 3. Character from "Hamlet" | PAILEOH |
| 4. Found in the sea or a tub | GENOPS |

**CLUE:** Very impressive

**BONUS** ◯◯◯◯◯◯◯

How to play    Complete the crossword puzzle by looking at the clues and unscrambling the answers. When the puzzle is complete, unscramble the circled letters to solve the BONUS.

# PUZZLE #29

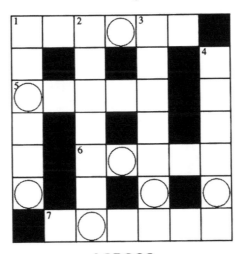

## JUMBLE CROSSWORDS™

### ACROSS

| CLUE | ANSWER |
|------|--------|
| 1. An island | THITIA |
| 5. Proverb | GAAED |
| 6. Lift or throw with effort | VAEEH |
| 7. County in W. Scotland | GRALLY |

### DOWN

| CLUE | ANSWER |
|------|--------|
| 1. Ending in disaster | ICARTG |
| 2. A flowering plant | TREHAHE |
| 3. *Physical* _____ | PREAYHT |
| 4. Writer George | LWROLE |

**CLUE:** This is usually cheaper

## BONUS

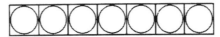

**How to play**  Complete the crossword puzzle by looking at the clues and unscrambling the answers. When the puzzle is complete, unscramble the circled letters to solve the BONUS.

30

# JUMBLE CROSSWORDS™

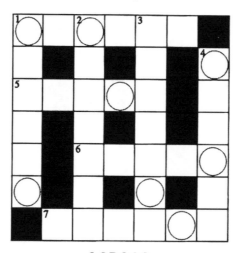

## ACROSS

| CLUE | ANSWER |
|------|--------|
| 1. A "Woman's" first name | D R O W E N |
| 5. Pointed | D I M A E |
| 6. Harder to finder | E R R R A |
| 7. Evaded | E D L E D U |

## DOWN

| CLUE | ANSWER |
|------|--------|
| 1. Plentiful amount | T E W L A H |
| 2. "1" is one | M A N U E L R |
| 3. Lasted | D R E U D N E |
| 4. Changed direction | R V E D E E |

**CLUE:** Anytime

BONUS

How to play — Complete the crossword puzzle by looking at the clues and unscrambling the answers. When the puzzle is complete, unscramble the circled letters to solve the BONUS.

# PUZZLE #31

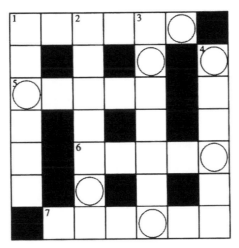

## JUMBLE CROSSWORDS™

### ACROSS

| CLUE | ANSWER |
|------|--------|
| 1. Follow and watch | SWOHDA |
| 5. Musical symbols | STEON |
| 6. Concur | ERGAE |
| 7. Notice | TTEECD |

### DOWN

| CLUE | ANSWER |
|------|--------|
| 1. Elder | SNIROE |
| 2. Put into action | CTATAEU |
| 3. Watch | VSBOEER |
| 4. *Take _____* | FEETCF |

**CLUE:** You can get caught *in* this

## BONUS

**How to play** Complete the crossword puzzle by looking at the clues and unscrambling the answers. When the puzzle is complete, unscramble the circled letters to solve the BONUS.

32

## JUMBLE CROSSWORDS™

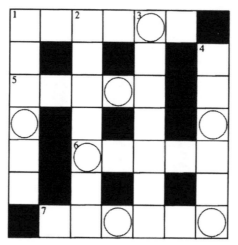

### ACROSS

| CLUE | ANSWER |
|---|---|
| 1. Extravagant | S V A L H I |
| 5. A potato is one | B R E T U |
| 6. Stand | A E I R S |
| 7. Scattered | S T E N R W |

### DOWN

| CLUE | ANSWER |
|---|---|
| 1. "_____ Weapon" | H A T L E L |
| 2. Full of vigor or energy | T A N R I V B |
| 3. Endure | S E I U V R V |
| 4. Trainee | T I N R E N |

**CLUE:** This *Bill* played a popular "Jim"

**BONUS**

How to play — Complete the crossword puzzle by looking at the clues and unscrambling the answers. When the puzzle is complete, unscramble the circled letters to solve the BONUS.

JUMBLE CROSSWORDS™

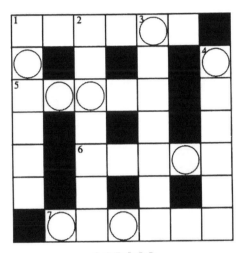

### ACROSS

| CLUE | ANSWER |
|------|--------|
| 1. *Stewart's* first name | HATRAM |
| 5. "Shout's" partner | TTSIW |
| 6. A fish | TEMLS |
| 7. Pushed in | NETEDD |

### DOWN

| CLUE | ANSWER |
|------|--------|
| 1. Reason | TIMEOV |
| 2. Put forth again | RSSEEIU |
| 3. Highest in temperature | STHTTOE |
| 4. Sequenced on paper | DILETS |

**CLUE:** Sometimes used like *easier*

BONUS

How to play — Complete the crossword puzzle by looking at the clues and unscrambling the answers. When the puzzle is complete, unscramble the circled letters to solve the BONUS.

# JUMBLE CROSSWORDS™

## ACROSS

| CLUE | | ANSWER |
|------|---|--------|
| 1. | A *magic* _____ | CRATEP |
| 5. | A capital | SNITU |
| 6. | Incompetent | PENIT |
| 7. | Goverment bureau | ACGYNE |

## DOWN

| CLUE | | ANSWER |
|------|---|--------|
| 1. | Oranges, lemons, etc. | STURCI |
| 2. | _____ *water* | NRGNINU |
| 3. | _____ *half* | STNREEA |
| 4. | Composition in verse | YEPRTO |

**CLUE:** Some say this can't be *stopped*

**BONUS**

How to play    Complete the crossword puzzle by looking at the clues and unscrambling the answers. When the puzzle is complete, unscramble the circled letters to solve the BONUS.

# PUZZLE #35

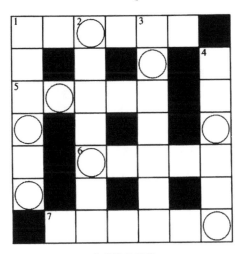

## JUMBLE CROSSWORDS™

### ACROSS

| CLUE | | ANSWER |
|------|--|--------|
| 1. '_____ Crosswords' | | BELMUJ |
| 5. D.Q.'s brother | | DYNRA |
| 6. A claw | | NOTLA |
| 7. This comes in a *box* | | NOYRAC |

### DOWN

| CLUE | | ANSWER |
|------|--|--------|
| 1. A breed of cattle | | SJEERY |
| 2. Screen | | TRONMOI |
| 3. Earned trust, faith | | OTAYYLL |
| 4. A TV "Frank" | | NNNCOA |

**CLUE:** *In* and *out*

**BONUS**

**How to play** Complete the crossword puzzle by looking at the clues and unscrambling the answers. When the puzzle is complete, unscramble the circled letters to solve the BONUS.

# JUMBLE CROSSWORDS™

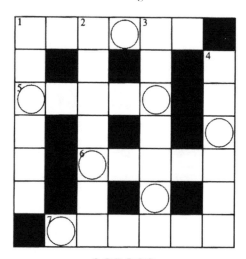

## ACROSS

| CLUE | | ANSWER |
|------|---|--------|
| 1. | "_____ Affair" | AYLIMF |
| 5. | A famous 37th | NNIOX |
| 6. | To make into law | CANTE |
| 7. | Around the longest | STEDOL |

## DOWN

| CLUE | | ANSWER |
|------|---|--------|
| 1. | _____ bender | DRENFE |
| 2. | A TV 'Smart' | LEXWAML |
| 3. | Descent | NILEEGA |
| 4. | Seven | TTEEPS |

**CLUE:** Sometimes done in *grand* fashion

**BONUS**

How to play  Complete the crossword puzzle by looking at the clues and unscrambling the answers. When the puzzle is complete, unscramble the circled letters to solve the BONUS.

# JUMBLE CROSSWORDS™

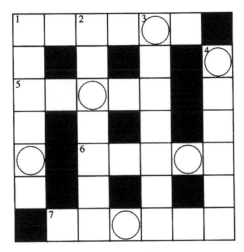

## ACROSS

| CLUE | ANSWER |
|------|--------|
| 1. Become aware | TINCEO |
| 5. Found in China | DAANP |
| 6. More | TARXE |
| 7. Deprive, extreme hunger | RATSEV |

## DOWN

| CLUE | ANSWER |
|------|--------|
| 1. In Florida or Italy | SPANEL |
| 2. A change in course | NATTGNE |
| 3. Pointless talk | RECTAHT |
| 4. Front | DACEAF |

**CLUE:** This takes up approx. 210,000 square miles

## BONUS ○○○○○○

**How to play** Complete the crossword puzzle by looking at the clues and unscrambling the answers. When the puzzle is complete, unscramble the circled letters to solve the BONUS.

# #38

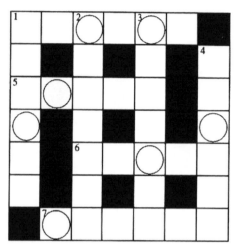

## JUMBLE CROSSWORDS™

### ACROSS

| CLUE | ANSWER |
|------|--------|
| 1. Found in Europe | L O P D A N |
| 5. *The Indigo _____* | S L I G R |
| 6. This has strings | O C L E L |
| 7. Elegant | S Y C A S L |

### DOWN

| CLUE | ANSWER |
|------|--------|
| 1. Far East temple | A G A D O P |
| 2. Having the form of a song | C L A Y R L I |
| 3. Snuggles | S N T E E L S |
| 4. A covering | P A C Y O N |

**CLUE:** After Buchanan, before Johnson

BONUS

**How to play** Complete the crossword puzzle by looking at the clues and unscrambling the answers. When the puzzle is complete, unscramble the circled letters to solve the BONUS.

# JUMBLE CROSSWORDS™

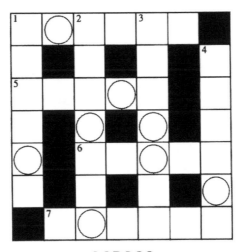

## ACROSS

| CLUE | ANSWER |
|------|--------|
| 1. A _____ plant | TOOTMA |
| 5. Cuban dance | GANCO |
| 6. Lubricated | EODIL |
| 7. Access | RETNEE |

## DOWN

| CLUE | ANSWER |
|------|--------|
| 1. Jeff Bridges role | RECUTK |
| 2. Storm | OOONNSM |
| 3. This can be pulled | RATEIRL |
| 4. A dessert | AENUDS |

**CLUE:** This can be *graded*

BONUS

How to play  Complete the crossword puzzle by looking at the clues and unscrambling the answers. When the puzzle is complete, unscramble the circled letters to solve the BONUS.

# #40

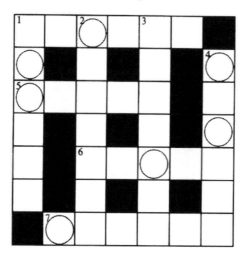

JUMBLE CROSSWORDS™

### ACROSS

| CLUE | ANSWER |
|------|--------|
| 1. Taken in a fairway | D T I S O V |
| 5. "Super" fast | S C I N O |
| 6. Feudal lord | G E E L I |
| 7. An aromatic tree | S M A L A B |

### DOWN

| CLUE | ANSWER |
|------|--------|
| 1. Hurried | H E D S A D |
| 2. Climbing orchid | L L V N A A I |
| 3. *Airline* _____ | K I T T E S C |
| 4. Make up for | M E D E E R |

**CLUE:** *Quickly, suddenly* and *hurriedly*

BONUS

**How to play**  Complete the crossword puzzle by looking at the clues and unscrambling the answers. When the puzzle is complete, unscramble the circled letters to solve the BONUS.

# 41

## JUMBLE CROSSWORDS™

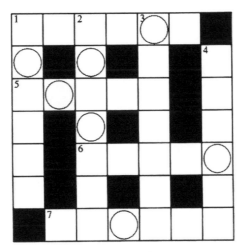

### ACROSS

| CLUE | ANSWER |
|------|--------|
| 1. *Brook's* first name | T R E F S O |
| 5. _____ *Clubs* | S N I L O |
| 6. Burns' sidekick | A N E L L |
| 7. Sluggish | N L E E D A |

### DOWN

| CLUE | ANSWER |
|------|--------|
| 1. Camera lens screen | T R E F L I |
| 2. _____ *space* | G R A T O E S |
| 3. Prepared, stored | S L I N D E E |
| 4. Flag | N N N O P E |

**CLUE:** A reason to keep going

## BONUS

**How to play** Complete the crossword puzzle by looking at the clues and unscrambling the answers. When the puzzle is complete, unscramble the circled letters to solve the BONUS.

# PUZZLE

# #42

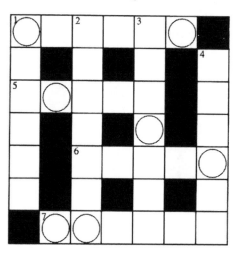

## JUMBLE CROSSWORDS™

### ACROSS

| CLUE | | ANSWER |
|------|---|--------|
| 1. | The "g" in mpg | LAGNOL |
| 5. | *Williams* first name | BORIN |
| 6. | This has *legs* | BLATE |
| 7. | Painting on moist plaster | FOCSER |

### DOWN

| CLUE | | ANSWER |
|------|---|--------|
| 1. | Famous for its aroma | RACLIG |
| 2. | Found in an ocean | LREOTBS |
| 3. | Large volume, collection | BINSUMO |
| 4. | A type of pavillion | BAGZOE |

**CLUE:** Unknown

**BONUS**

**How to play** Complete the crossword puzzle by looking at the clues and unscrambling the answers. When the puzzle is complete, unscramble the circled letters to solve the BONUS.

43

# JUMBLE CROSSWORDS™

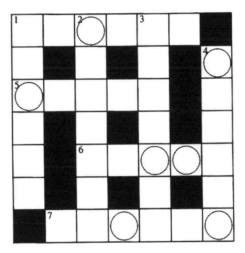

### ACROSS

| CLUE | ANSWER |
|------|--------|
| 1. Famous *Harry* | NATMUR |
| 5. Woman's name | NEERI |
| 6. Extreme | TUARL |
| 7. The answer _____ me | DSLEEU |

### DOWN

| CLUE | ANSWER |
|------|--------|
| 1. Similar to hunger | STRITH |
| 2. Uneven or variable | QLAEUUN |
| 3. Prevented | TRAEEDV |
| 4. Found on flowers | STAPEL |

**CLUE:** *Hot _____*

# BONUS

How to play — Complete the crossword puzzle by looking at the clues and unscrambling the answers. When the puzzle is complete, unscramble the circled letters to solve the BONUS.

# JUMBLE CROSSWORDS™

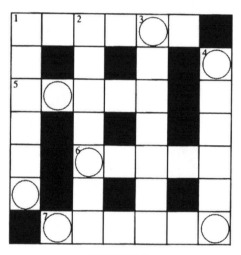

## ACROSS

| CLUE | ANSWER |
|------|--------|
| 1. "Ed" or "Rogers" | TRIMES |
| 5. Rent | SLEEA |
| 6. _____ down | RPSSE |
| 7. *Jodie's* last name | TROFES |

## DOWN

| CLUE | ANSWER |
|------|--------|
| 1. A cereal grass | MLTELI |
| 2. *Beatty* movie | OSOPMHA |
| 3. Component of a whole | LNETMEE |
| 4. An official, examiner | SRONEC |

**CLUE:** After *picture* or before *score*

**BONUS**

How to play  Complete the crossword puzzle by looking at the clues and unscrambling the answers. When the puzzle is complete, unscramble the circled letters to solve the BONUS.

45

# JUMBLE CROSSWORDS™

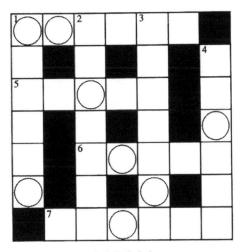

### ACROSS

| CLUE | ANSWER |
|------|--------|
| 1. A dazed condition | CRTNAE |
| 5. Pointed nails | SKTCA |
| 6. Most powerful members | EETLI |
| 7. Made amends | DAEONT |

### DOWN

| CLUE | ANSWER |
|------|--------|
| 1. "Mr. Roarke's" sidekick | AOOTTT |
| 2. _____ Egypt | TANNECI |
| 3. Soften the effects | CSOINHU |
| 4. Rely | DDNEEP |

**CLUE:** Etiquette

**BONUS**

**How to play** Complete the crossword puzzle by looking at the clues and unscrambling the answers. When the puzzle is complete, unscramble the circled letters to solve the BONUS.

# #46

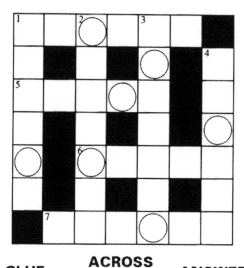

## ACROSS

| CLUE | ANSWER |
|------|--------|
| 1. Satirical imitation | DYRPOA |
| 5. A fictional sidekick | NRIOB |
| 6. Free from confusion | RECAL |
| 7. Flag | RNENAB |

## DOWN

| CLUE | ANSWER |
|------|--------|
| 1. Copy without permission | PTERIA |
| 2. "Cheers" character | ABEECCR |
| 3. Prison | GNDOENU |
| 4. Closer | RREEAN |

**CLUE:** You don't have to have paper to *draw* one

BONUS

How to play    Complete the crossword puzzle by looking at the clues and unscrambling the answers. When the puzzle is complete, unscramble the circled letters to solve the BONUS.

**#47**

# JUMBLE CROSSWORDS™

## ACROSS

| CLUE | ANSWER |
|------|--------|
| 1. _____ down | LKUBEC |
| 5. Leave | MSRAC |
| 6. Straight _____ | DAAEH |
| 7. Mixture of proteins | TLNEUG |

## DOWN

| CLUE | ANSWER |
|------|--------|
| 1. A chess piece | SPHIOB |
| 2. Cut short | LCITRAU |
| 3. Playing lightly, flickering | BLETNAM |
| 4. _____ off | NOODRC |

**CLUE:** Show

**BONUS** ○○○○○○○○

**How to play** Complete the crossword puzzle by looking at the clues and unscrambling the answers. When the puzzle is complete, unscramble the circled letters to solve the BONUS.

48

# #48

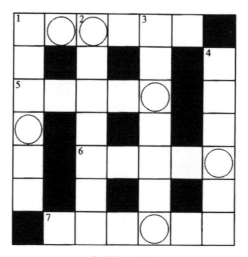

## JUMBLE CROSSWORDS™

### ACROSS

| CLUE | | ANSWER |
|------|--|--------|
| 1. | Vain | L F E U I T |
| 5. | Estimate | S G E U S |
| 6. | Woman's name | A E C R I |
| 7. | Judged | D G G A U E |

### DOWN

| CLUE | | ANSWER |
|------|--|--------|
| 1. | _____ out | F E R G I U |
| 2. | *Mother* _____ | S T E E H A R |
| 3. | Continuing | T G A L S N I |
| 4. | *Ron's* last name | D A W O R H |

**CLUE: "8"**

## BONUS

**How to play** — Complete the crossword puzzle by looking at the clues and unscrambling the answers. When the puzzle is complete, unscramble the circled letters to solve the BONUS.

# JUMBLE CROSSWORDS™

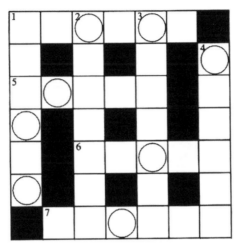

## ACROSS

| CLUE | ANSWER |
|------|--------|
| 1. Goals | SDAREM |
| 5. Indispensable | TLVIA |
| 6. _____ *Moorehead* | SGENA |
| 7. Make beloved | DRANEE |

## DOWN

| CLUE | ANSWER |
|------|--------|
| 1. Contrive, create | EESDVI |
| 2. Go aboard | NEINART |
| 3. *Griffith's* first name | MEENIAL |
| 4. Roman general | CRSEAE |

**CLUE:** Remedy

BONUS

How to play — Complete the crossword puzzle by looking at the clues and unscrambling the answers. When the puzzle is complete, unscramble the circled letters to solve the BONUS.

# JUMBLE CROSSWORDS™

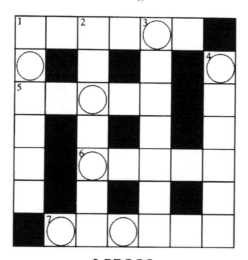

## ACROSS

| CLUE | ANSWER |
| --- | --- |
| 1. *Murdoch's* first name | TRRPUE |
| 5. _____ *Hamilton* | DANIL |
| 6. Provide food | CRETA |
| 7. Scarcity | HDTERA |

## DOWN

| CLUE | ANSWER |
| --- | --- |
| 1. Remaining parts | SCRILE |
| 2. Flair | CAPEHNA |
| 3. Used for cooking meat | TRARESO |
| 4. Found in rice, corn, etc. | SCRATH |

**CLUE:** Kelly, Rogers, etc.

**BONUS**

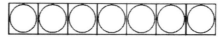

How to play   Complete the crossword puzzle by looking at the clues and unscrambling the answers. When the puzzle is complete, unscramble the circled letters to solve the BONUS.

51

# #51

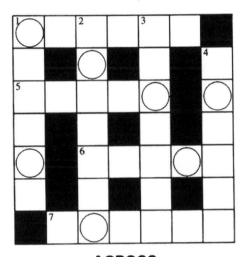

## JUMBLE CROSSWORDS™

### ACROSS

| CLUE | | ANSWER |
|---|---|---|
| 1. | Portray | TIPCED |
| 5. | Last Greek letter | GAMOE |
| 6. | *Within* prefix | TRANI |
| 7. | _____ *Gobel* | EOGREG |

### DOWN

| CLUE | | ANSWER |
|---|---|---|
| 1. | Sleepy | YDSRWO |
| 2. | This supports a conclusion | SIPMEER |
| 3. | Fraternity branch | PRETCAH |
| 4. | Threatening person | CEENAM |

**CLUE:** You are one of these

## BONUS

**How to play** — Complete the crossword puzzle by looking at the clues and unscrambling the answers. When the puzzle is complete, unscramble the circled letters to solve the BONUS.

# #52

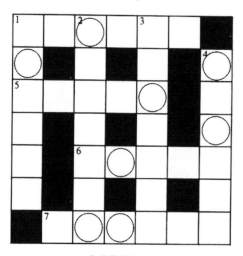

## JUMBLE CROSSWORDS™

### ACROSS

| CLUE | | ANSWER |
|------|--|--------|
| 1. _____ in place | | F Y L I M R |
| 5. Put back to zero | | S E E T R |
| 6. Thrown as part of a game | | S T A R D |
| 7. Repeat | | A E Y R L P |

### DOWN

| CLUE | | ANSWER |
|------|--|--------|
| 1. A weasel | | R E F T E R |
| 2. Something that remains | | S E R D E I U |
| 3. To the side | | T R E A L L A |
| 4. Fancy or stylish | | S D Y S R E |

**CLUE:** "Over," in *over and over*

**BONUS**

**How to play** Complete the crossword puzzle by looking at the clues and unscrambling the answers. When the puzzle is complete, unscramble the circled letters to solve the BONUS.

# 53

## JUMBLE CROSSWORDS™

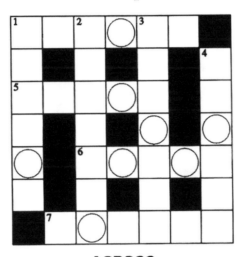

### ACROSS

| CLUE | ANSWER |
|------|--------|
| 1. "Rhoda" actress | PHRARE |
| 5. Bungle | HBCOT |
| 6. The top of the _____ | HNTNI |
| 7. You can apply for one | TTEAPN |

### DOWN

| CLUE | ANSWER |
|------|--------|
| 1. The "_____ Telescope" | BLEBUH |
| 2. Circular hall | TRDAUON |
| 3. Improve | CNNHEAE |
| 4. Final outcome | STOUPH |

**CLUE:** *Hamilton, Wellington* and *Sofia*

**BONUS**

How to play — Complete the crossword puzzle by looking at the clues and unscrambling the answers. When the puzzle is complete, unscramble the circled letters to solve the BONUS.

# #54

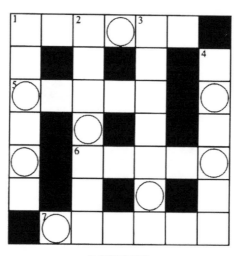

## JUMBLE CROSSWORDS™

### ACROSS

| CLUE | | ANSWER |
|---|---|---|
| 1. "Flash _____" | | N O O D R G |
| 5. Filthy | | S N Y T A |
| 6. To force away | | L E E P R |
| 7. Announce, proclaim | | L A R D E H |

### DOWN

| CLUE | | ANSWER |
|---|---|---|
| 1. "Grant's" first name | | G R E G N I |
| 2. Hold | | R R E E E V S |
| 3. *Dukakis'* first name | | P O L Y A M I |
| 4. A simple song | | L A B D A L |

**CLUE:** Usually bigger and bolder, easy to spot

BONUS

**How to play**   Complete the crossword puzzle by looking at the clues and unscrambling the answers. When the puzzle is complete, unscramble the circled letters to solve the BONUS.

55

# JUMBLE CROSSWORDS™

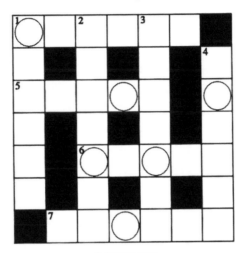

## ACROSS

| CLUE | ANSWER |
|------|--------|
| 1. Famous river | STEAMH |
| 5. *Kelly* or *Jones* | CARGE |
| 6. _____ pollution | OSENI |
| 7. Periods, steps | GATESS |

## DOWN

| CLUE | ANSWER |
|------|--------|
| 1. Marked | GDAETG |
| 2. Contrary to | STANGAI |
| 3. Latter part of the day | INNVGEE |
| 4. European capital | SHANET |

**CLUE:** Together

## BONUS

**How to play**  Complete the crossword puzzle by looking at the clues and unscrambling the answers. When the puzzle is complete, unscramble the circled letters to solve the BONUS.

56

# #56

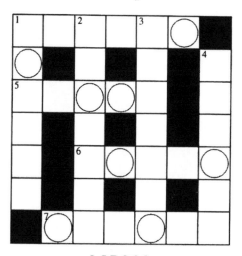

## JUMBLE CROSSWORDS™

### ACROSS

| CLUE | ANSWER |
|------|--------|
| 1. Luck | C C E N A H |
| 5. _____ rule | E S D L I |
| 6. Body joint | L E K N A |
| 7. Legal _____ | D R E E N T |

### DOWN

| CLUE | ANSWER |
|------|--------|
| 1. Practice, habit | U S T O C M |
| 2. Alive | T A I M N A E |
| 3. Double _____ | C K E E D C H |
| 4. Come into public view | R A P P E A |

**CLUE:** One way you will never see these puzzles

**BONUS**

**How to play**  Complete the crossword puzzle by looking at the clues and unscrambling the answers. When the puzzle is complete, unscramble the circled letters to solve the BONUS.

# JUMBLE CROSSWORDS™

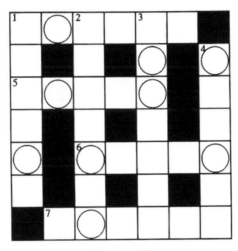

## ACROSS

| CLUE | ANSWER |
|------|--------|
| 1. To steal cattle | R L E T S U |
| 5. Freight | G R O A C |
| 6. Attempted | D T I E R |
| 7. Unkempt | G H Y A S G |

## DOWN

| CLUE | ANSWER |
|------|--------|
| 1. Auto-maker's fear | L E L C A R |
| 2. _____ limo | S H R C T T E |
| 3. Appearing, ominous | N L M O G I O |
| 4. Lethal | D Y D L E A |

**CLUE:** It takes time for you to reach this

BONUS

**How to play** Complete the crossword puzzle by looking at the clues and unscrambling the answers. When the puzzle is complete, unscramble the circled letters to solve the BONUS.

# #58

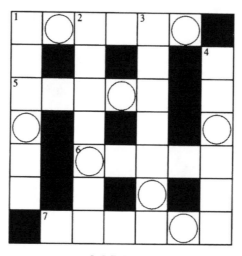

# JUMBLE CROSSWORDS™

## ACROSS

| CLUE | ANSWER |
|------|--------|
| 1. Conundrum | DLREID |
| 5. Groups, factions | CTESS |
| 6. *Weaver* film | NILEA |
| 7. Distance | HETGNL |

## DOWN

| CLUE | ANSWER |
|------|--------|
| 1. Dwell | DISEER |
| 2. Announce | CALEERD |
| 3. Long _____ | NLIATGS |
| 4. Wince, recoil | NIHFCL |

**CLUE:** Begin

**BONUS**

**How to play** Complete the crossword puzzle by looking at the clues and unscrambling the answers. When the puzzle is complete, unscramble the circled letters to solve the BONUS.

#59

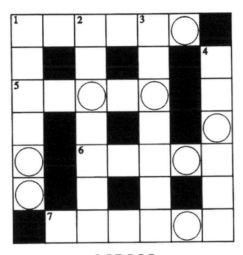

JUMBLE CROSSWORDS™

### ACROSS

| CLUE | ANSWER |
|------|--------|
| 1. Critic | NUTIPD |
| 5. Unpredictable, risky | CYDEI |
| 6. _____ *cell* | LOSRA |
| 7. Wild, thoughtless | CMPDAA |

### DOWN

| CLUE | ANSWER |
|------|--------|
| 1. Found on most pianos | DSLEPA |
| 2. Island capital | SCINAIO |
| 3. Pleasing | CLDIILY |
| 4. Catch, snare | RTENPA |

**CLUE:** This can bring about a significant change

BONUS

**How to play** Complete the crossword puzzle by looking at the clues and unscrambling the answers. When the puzzle is complete, unscramble the circled letters to solve the BONUS.

# #60

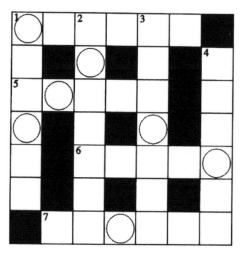

# JUMBLE CROSSWORDS™

## ACROSS

| CLUE | | ANSWER |
|------|--|--------|
| 1. | Gather | STREUM |
| 5. | Fragment, remnant | CLIRE |
| 6. | Fictional winged boy | DPCIU |
| 7. | But, except | SLENUS |

## DOWN

| CLUE | | ANSWER |
|------|--|--------|
| 1. | Low indistinct sound | RRUUMM |
| 2. | "_____ Valley" | SNOCLII |
| 3. | Fugitive | EEEPACS |
| 4. | Mass departure | SOXDUE |

**CLUE:** Problem

**BONUS**

How to play    Complete the crossword puzzle by looking at the clues and unscrambling the answers. When the puzzle is complete, unscramble the circled letters to solve the BONUS.

# PUZZLE #61

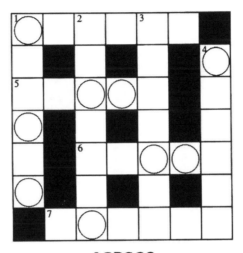

## JUMBLE CROSSWORDS™

### ACROSS

| CLUE | ANSWER |
|------|--------|
| 1. This has its own *London* | D A A A N C |
| 5. You can sing this | S L E U B |
| 6. _____ *transit* | D R I A P |
| 7. Projecting rim | G E N A L F |

### DOWN

| CLUE | ANSWER |
|------|--------|
| 1. Its symbol is "Co" | C A O T B L |
| 2. "Star Trek's" *Zone* | T R A N U L E |
| 3. Used with a broom | N A P D U T S |
| 4. Waste time | W A D E L D |

**CLUE:** Repeat   **CLUE:** Repeat

BONUS

How to play   Complete the crossword puzzle by looking at the clues and unscrambling the answers. When the puzzle is complete, unscramble the circled letters to solve the BONUS.

62

# #62

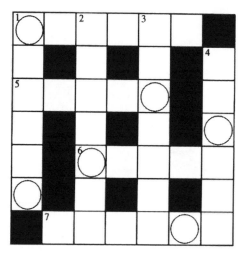

## JUMBLE CROSSWORDS™

**ACROSS**

| CLUE | | ANSWER |
|------|---|--------|
| 1. | Dressing table | TYNIAV |
| 5. | Age, cure | NIPER |
| 6. | _____ *jack* | INNOU |
| 7. | Canine shelter | EENLNK |

**DOWN**

| CLUE | | ANSWER |
|------|---|--------|
| 1. | Beneficial quality | TRIVEU |
| 2. | Roman god | PENETNU |
| 3. | Stress | SNETINO |
| 4. | Burrow | NLTEUN |

**CLUE:** Three on this side and four on that side

## BONUS

**How to play** Complete the crossword puzzle by looking at the clues and unscrambling the answers. When the puzzle is complete, unscramble the circled letters to solve the BONUS.

# #63

## JUMBLE CROSSWORDS™

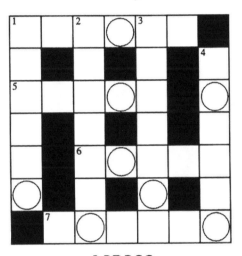

### ACROSS

| CLUE | ANSWER |
|------|--------|
| 1. A tool | LETOWR |
| 5. *Kathy's* last name | STABE |
| 6. Reduce in intensity | TABEA |
| 7. Edible plant | YCREEL |

### DOWN

| CLUE | ANSWER |
|------|--------|
| 1. Lists | BLATSE |
| 2. Anger | GERATUO |
| 3. Capture | SNANERE |
| 4. One and only | SLOYLE |

**CLUE:** Yours can be *raised*

BONUS

**How to play** Complete the crossword puzzle by looking at the clues and unscrambling the answers. When the puzzle is complete, unscramble the circled letters to solve the BONUS.

JUMBLE CROSSWORDS™

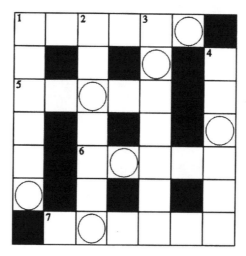

## ACROSS

| CLUE | ANSWER |
|------|--------|
| 1. Make harmless | M A R S I D |
| 5. _____ *life* | F E L S H |
| 6. "Rosa" is its highest point | L Y T I A |
| 7. Scheduled | S D E L T A |

## DOWN

| CLUE | ANSWER |
|------|--------|
| 1. Repudiate | S D I N O W |
| 2. Specific | C L A S P I E |
| 3. Change direction | R T C A R E F |
| 4. Followed | Y O E E D B |

**CLUE:** "He" is one, but "She" is not

## BONUS

How to play   Complete the crossword puzzle by looking at the clues and unscrambling the answers. When the puzzle is complete, unscramble the circled letters to solve the BONUS.

# JUMBLE CROSSWORDS

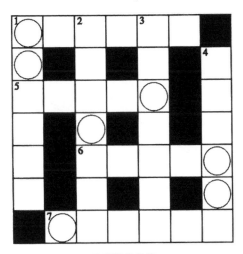

## ACROSS

| CLUE | | ANSWER |
|------|--|--------|
| 1. | *Wichita's* home | SNAASK |
| 5. | Type of structure | RWETO |
| 6. | *Fluid* _____ | NOEUC |
| 7. | Directs | RETSES |

## DOWN

| CLUE | | ANSWER |
|------|--|--------|
| 1. | Young cat | NIKETT |
| 2. | U.S. seaport | PRENOWT |
| 3. | Orchestrate | AAGENRR |
| 4. | Muscles | SPICEB |

**CLUE:** "Jonas Grumby"

BONUS **THE** ◯◯◯◯◯◯◯

**How to play**  Complete the crossword puzzle by looking at the clues and unscrambling the answers. When the puzzle is complete, unscramble the circled letters to solve the BONUS.

# JUMBLE CROSSWORDS™

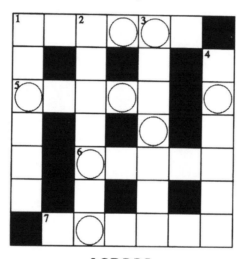

## ACROSS

| CLUE | ANSWER |
|------|--------|
| 1. African country | GANALO |
| 5. Vigorous criticism | STABL |
| 6. Found on a wall | LAMRU |
| 7. Luxuries | SLIRLF |

## DOWN

| CLUE | ANSWER |
|------|--------|
| 1. Eddie's last name | ARTEBL |
| 2. Language rules | MARGRAM |
| 3. True to fact | LLEIART |
| 4. Knocks over | SLIPSL |

**CLUE:** 1+1=? and a broken radiator

BONUS

**How to play** Complete the crossword puzzle by looking at the clues and unscrambling the answers. When the puzzle is complete, unscramble the circled letters to solve the BONUS.

67

# #67

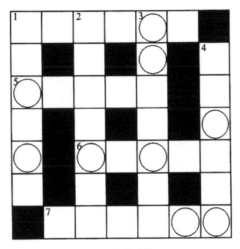

## JUMBLE CROSSWORDS™

### ACROSS

| CLUE | | ANSWER |
|------|---|--------|
| 1. | Conceded | ERAGDE |
| 5. | Conical tent | PEEET |
| 6. | *Doubleday's* first name | RABEN |
| 7. | Famous "Magician" | LIMREN |

### DOWN

| CLUE | | ANSWER |
|------|---|--------|
| 1. | Director's shout | NOTAIC |
| 2. | Switch | PLEREAC |
| 3. | Without end | EELANRT |
| 4. | Customer | TAPNOR |

**CLUE:** It doesn't cost you anything to *pay* this

BONUS ◯◯◯◯◯◯◯◯◯

**How to play** Complete the crossword puzzle by looking at the clues and unscrambling the answers. When the puzzle is complete, unscramble the circled letters to solve the BONUS.

# #68

## JUMBLE CROSSWORDS™

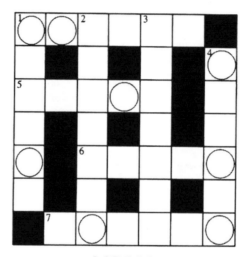

### ACROSS

| CLUE | ANSWER |
|------|--------|
| 1. _____ out | G I R E U F |
| 5. Loud sound | A G N L C |
| 6. Free from restraint | U E N I T |
| 7. Continuously | Y A S A L W |

### DOWN

| CLUE | ANSWER |
|------|--------|
| 1. Beauty treatment | L F A A I C |
| 2. Little by little | G L R D A A U |
| 3. Boat race | R A T E T A G |
| 4. *The _____ that be* | S P O R W E |

**CLUE:** Yours is yet to be determined

**BONUS**
2 WORDS

**How to play** Complete the crossword puzzle by looking at the clues and unscrambling the answers. When the puzzle is complete, unscramble the circled letters to solve the BONUS.

# #69

## JUMBLE CROSSWORDS™

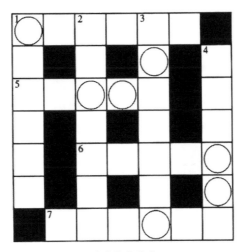

### ACROSS

| CLUE | ANSWER |
|------|--------|
| 1. *J.T.* movie | SARGEE |
| 5. Suspenseful events | MADAR |
| 6. Total, absolute | TRUET |
| 7. Top _____ | STEERC |

### DOWN

| CLUE | ANSWER |
|------|--------|
| 1. Device | TAGGDE |
| 2. Obliteration | RREESUA |
| 3. Splash | STAREPT |
| 4. "Bugs'" favorite | TAROCR |

**CLUE:** You can watch one kind or hold another

## BONUS

**How to play** Complete the crossword puzzle by looking at the clues and unscrambling the answers. When the puzzle is complete, unscramble the circled letters to solve the BONUS.

## JUMBLE CROSSWORDS™

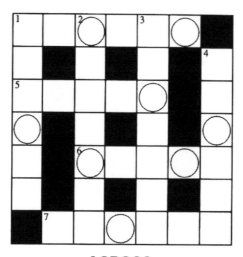

### ACROSS

| CLUE | ANSWER |
|------|--------|
| 1. *Good* or *bad* _____ | C A I V E D |
| 5. Discussion | M U F R O |
| 6. Perfection | L A D E I |
| 7. Situation, condition | T T U A S S |

### DOWN

| CLUE | ANSWER |
|------|--------|
| 1. Declare, ratify | F F M R A I |
| 2. Judgment | C I D E T V R |
| 3. Remark | T N M O C M E |
| 4. Southern U.S. city | S L A D A L |

**CLUE:** 'I would love to hear from you ____ ____.'

**BONUS**
2 WORDS

**How to play**   Complete the crossword puzzle by looking at the clues and unscrambling the answers. When the puzzle is complete, unscramble the circled letters to solve the BONUS.

71

# JUMBLE CROSSWORDS™

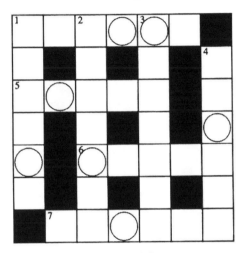

## ACROSS

| CLUE | ANSWER |
|------|--------|
| 1. Take away | TEDDCU |
| 5. Surmise | FNREI |
| 6. Unit of measurement | CONEU |
| 7. Kept, retained | RESTOD |

## DOWN

| CLUE | ANSWER |
|------|--------|
| 1. Of delicate beauty | TYNAID |
| 2. Thaw | STROFDE |
| 3. A public officer | ROCRENO |
| 4. Surpass | EEEDCX |

**CLUE:** Although not a "white meat," this does have white meat

## BONUS

**How to play** Complete the crossword puzzle by looking at the clues and unscrambling the answers. When the puzzle is complete, unscramble the circled letters to solve the BONUS.

# JUMBLE CROSSWORDS™

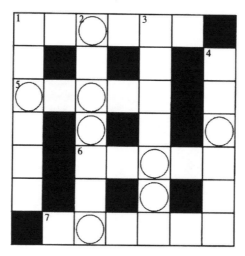

## ACROSS

| CLUE | | ANSWER |
|------|---|--------|
| 1. | _____ figure | THREAF |
| 5. | This requires a signature | SLEEA |
| 6. | Lower half covering | STANP |
| 7. | 1st, 2nd or 3rd _____ | EGEDER |

## DOWN

| CLUE | | ANSWER |
|------|---|--------|
| 1. | A crime | NOLEYF |
| 2. | Crush, destroy | PAMRELT |
| 3. | *Roosevelt* or *Rigby* | EERANOL |
| 4. | Chase | SPUUER |

**CLUE:** A North American city

BONUS

**How to play**   Complete the crossword puzzle by looking at the clues and unscrambling the answers. When the puzzle is complete, unscramble the circled letters to solve the BONUS.

# #73

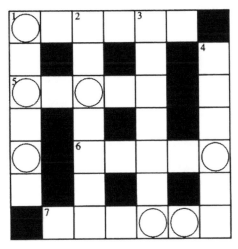

## JUMBLE CROSSWORDS™

### ACROSS

| CLUE | ANSWER |
|------|--------|
| 1. Fall | NATMUU |
| 5. Procrastinate | LASTL |
| 6. *On the _____* | LOPWR |
| 7. Bad, shabby | YCURMM |

### DOWN

| CLUE | ANSWER |
|------|--------|
| 1. Take for granted | SASEUM |
| 2. "_____ John" | PRATREP |
| 3. McDowell's first name | LMMOACL |
| 4. Cable supporting wheel | LPYEUL |

**CLUE:** Man and a manatee

## BONUS

**How to play** Complete the crossword puzzle by looking at the clues and unscrambling the answers. When the puzzle is complete, unscramble the circled letters to solve the BONUS.

# JUMBLE CROSSWORDS™

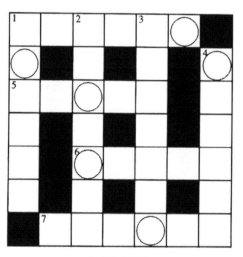

## ACROSS

| CLUE | ANSWER |
|------|--------|
| 1. Flowering plant | V L O R E C |
| 5. _____ *membrane* | S C U U M |
| 6. Event area | R E N A A |
| 7. *Greek* _____ | D I N S O A |

## DOWN

| CLUE | ANSWER |
|------|--------|
| 1. Seen often | N O M O M C |
| 2. Type of farm | C H O R R D A |
| 3. _____ *Europe* | E N T E R S A |
| 4. Bother | S H A R S A |

**CLUE:** This can be a weight or a person

## BONUS

**How to play** Complete the crossword puzzle by looking at the clues and unscrambling the answers. When the puzzle is complete, unscramble the circled letters to solve the BONUS.

# PUZZLE #75

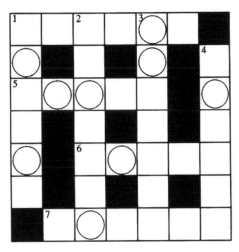

JUMBLE CROSSWORDS™

### ACROSS

| CLUE | ANSWER |
|---|---|
| 1. A bird or a country | KRYTUE |
| 5. Greek philosopher | OPALT |
| 6. Two times | CEWIT |
| 7. A meal | NURCHB |

### DOWN

| CLUE | ANSWER |
|---|---|
| 1. Exemplify | PITYYF |
| 2. Cooker | STEAROR |
| 3. You can *show* this | MOONITE |
| 4. Stalin's first name | SHPOJE |

**CLUE:** Christopher Jones was its captain

BONUS

**How to play** Complete the crossword puzzle by looking at the clues and unscrambling the answers. When the puzzle is complete, unscramble the circled letters to solve the BONUS.

76

# JUMBLE CROSSWORDS™

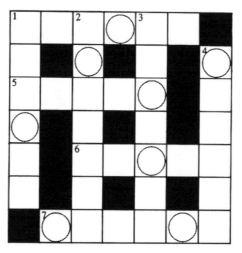

### ACROSS

| CLUE | | ANSWER |
|------|---|--------|
| 1. | Missing | STABNE |
| 5. | _____ answer | UNSOB |
| 6. | City in Texas | TRELY |
| 7. | Type of bed | LDARCE |

### DOWN

| CLUE | | ANSWER |
|------|---|--------|
| 1. | Reddish brown | ANRUUB |
| 2. | Government official | TRANSOE |
| 3. | Pressed closely | DEENLTS |
| 4. | Beginning | EUSCOR |

( )

**BONUS**

How to play — Complete the crossword puzzle by looking at the clues and unscrambling the answers. When the puzzle is complete, unscramble the circled letters to solve the BONUS.

# JUMBLE CROSSWORDS™

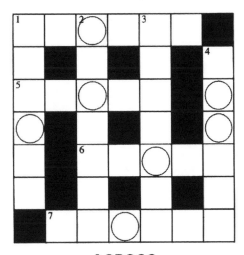

## ACROSS

| CLUE | ANSWER |
|---|---|
| 1. Verse composition | TOYPER |
| 5. Marked by falsehoods | GINYL |
| 6. A group or set | OTTCE |
| 7. "Dennis" was one | CMAEEN |

## DOWN

| CLUE | ANSWER |
|---|---|
| 1. *Jim* or *Robert* | MAPLER |
| 2. Installment, part | EEDSOIP |
| 3. Type of race | TAGATER |
| 4. Energetic activity | LETSUB |

**CLUE:** These can pass or be written down

**BONUS** ○○○○○○○

**How to play** Complete the crossword puzzle by looking at the clues and unscrambling the answers. When the puzzle is complete, unscramble the circled letters to solve the BONUS.

# PUZZLE #78

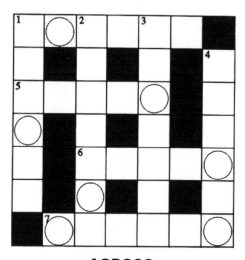

## JUMBLE CROSSWORDS™

### ACROSS

| CLUE | ANSWER |
|------|--------|
| 1. Examine | CRAESH |
| 5. Fossil resin | BRAME |
| 6. This might annoy you | ISONE |
| 7. Package | CLEPRA |

### DOWN

| CLUE | ANSWER |
|------|--------|
| 1. A work of art | TAUSTE |
| 2. European country | BILANAA |
| 3. _____ arrest | DRACCAI |
| 4. Attraction | PLEAPA |

**CLUE:** A broad classification

**BONUS** ○○○○○○○

**How to play** Complete the crossword puzzle by looking at the clues and unscrambling the answers. When the puzzle is complete, unscramble the circled letters to solve the BONUS.

#79

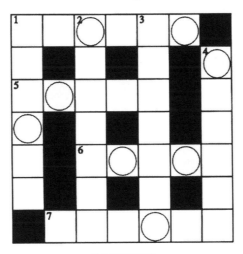

## JUMBLE CROSSWORDS™

### ACROSS

| CLUE | | ANSWER |
|------|---|--------|
| 1. | Type of sausage | MILAAS |
| 5. | Warning sound | NSERI |
| 6. | Placed by creditors | SNILE |
| 7. | A fuel | EELSID |

### DOWN

| CLUE | | ANSWER |
|------|---|--------|
| 1. | Seed of an herb | MSSAEE |
| 2. | Legendary singer | LLIEERO |
| 3. | D.J., M.N., P.T. and M.D. | SKONEME |
| 4. | Dangling ornament | STELAS |

CLUE: D.J., M.N., P.T., and M.D.

BONUS

**How to play** Complete the crossword puzzle by looking at the clues and unscrambling the answers. When the puzzle is complete, unscramble the circled letters to solve the BONUS.

# #80

## JUMBLE CROSSWORDS™

### ACROSS

| CLUE | | ANSWER |
|------|---|--------|
| 1. | Dressed up | MORLAF |
| 5. | Turn back to zero | STERE |
| 6. | _____ *city* | NIRNE |
| 7. | A fleet | DRAMAA |

### DOWN

| CLUE | | ANSWER |
|------|---|--------|
| 1. | Cultivator | RREMAF |
| 2. | More dangerous | RSIRIEK |
| 3. | Found on insects | NENANAT |
| 4. | A range of mountains | RARIES |

**CLUE:** Three of this show's four stars have first names starting with "J"

**BONUS** ○○○○○○○○

**How to play** Complete the crossword puzzle by looking at the clues and unscrambling the answers. When the puzzle is complete, unscramble the circled letters to solve the BONUS.

# JUMBLE CROSSWORDS™

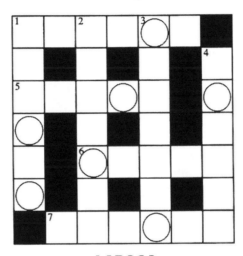

## ACROSS

| CLUE | ANSWER |
|------|--------|
| 1. Fantastic | PREBUS |
| 5. _____ and operated | WEDON |
| 6. Fictional "Madison" | CRASO |
| 7. Fexible, folding case | TELALW |

## DOWN

| CLUE | ANSWER |
|------|--------|
| 1. A tool | HELOVS |
| 2. "Box" owner | DRANAPO |
| 3. Extreme | CLADARI |
| 4. Variety of bird | TRAPRO |

**CLUE:** Total, end to end

BONUS

**How to play** Complete the crossword puzzle by looking at the clues and unscrambling the answers. When the puzzle is complete, unscramble the circled letters to solve the BONUS.

# PUZZLE #82

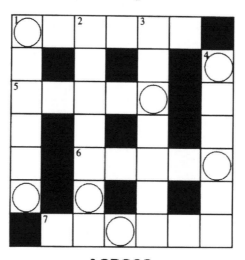

## JUMBLE CROSSWORDS™

### ACROSS

| CLUE | ANSWER |
|------|--------|
| 1. Reason to raise hand | W A S R E N |
| 5. Already over | N E D D E |
| 6. 3rd of 9 | T R H A E |
| 7. Rise | D A S N E C |

### DOWN

| CLUE | ANSWER |
|------|--------|
| 1. Get even | V E G N A E |
| 2. Something you feel | D S N S A S E |
| 3. Approve | S N O D E E R |
| 4. Moved angrily | H A L S D E |

**CLUE:** Did not go together

## BONUS

**How to play** Complete the crossword puzzle by looking at the clues and unscrambling the answers. When the puzzle is complete, unscramble the circled letters to solve the BONUS.

83

# #83

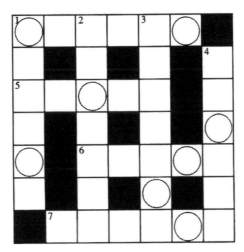

## JUMBLE CROSSWORDS™

### ACROSS

| CLUE | ANSWER |
|------|--------|
| 1. *Lawrence's* home | S K S N A A |
| 5. Pocket change | S M I D E |
| 6. Pluto's designation | T H I N N |
| 7. Cured | D E L E H A |

### DOWN

| CLUE | ANSWER |
|------|--------|
| 1. Small child | D D E K I I |
| 2. Candidate | E N E O N M I |
| 3. Collection of weapons | R A S L A N E |
| 4. Crushed | S M E D H A |

**CLUE:** *"One of my biggest fears"*

BONUS

How to play — Complete the crossword puzzle by looking at the clues and unscrambling the answers. When the puzzle is complete, unscramble the circled letters to solve the BONUS.

# JUMBLE CROSSWORDS™

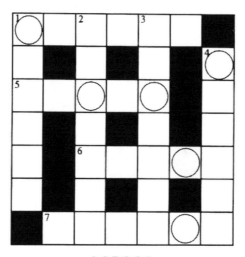

### ACROSS

| CLUE | ANSWER |
|---|---|
| 1. Like sadness | WOORSR |
| 5. *Leonard* _____ | OMNIY |
| 6. Used to make *sauce* | PLAPE |
| 7. This has a handle | UTAECP |

### DOWN

| CLUE | ANSWER |
|---|---|
| 1. Foot covering | SLAADN |
| 2. Violent action | GAMEPAR |
| 3. _____ *Games* | CYIMPLO |
| 4. Inactive | PLEAES |

**CLUE:** This is sometimes *given*

## BONUS ○○○○○○

**How to play** Complete the crossword puzzle by looking at the clues and unscrambling the answers. When the puzzle is complete, unscramble the circled letters to solve the BONUS.

# JUMBLE CROSSWORDS™

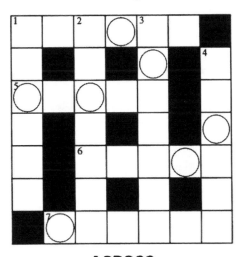

## ACROSS

| CLUE | ANSWER |
|------|--------|
| 1. Change | OYMIDF |
| 5. Used to pick up things | GNOST |
| 6. Similar to perfect | LADEI |
| 7. _____ electricity | SCITAT |

## DOWN

| CLUE | ANSWER |
|------|--------|
| 1. Procedure | THEMDO |
| 2. Associated with pain | STINTDE |
| 3. Sometimes the winner | STATSEF |
| 4. This has a strong smell | CLIGRA |

**CLUE:** A famous performer

**BONUS**

How to play   Complete the crossword puzzle by looking at the clues and unscrambling the answers. When the puzzle is complete, unscramble the circled letters to solve the BONUS.

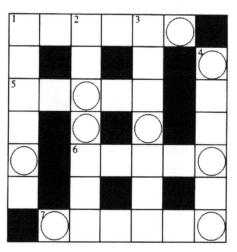

## JUMBLE CROSSWORDS™

### ACROSS

| CLUE | | ANSWER |
|------|---|--------|
| 1. | This | ZLEPZU |
| 5. | Unpleasent | TYNSA |
| 6. | Paperwork person | FLERI |
| 7. | Killed | DAYELS |

### DOWN

| CLUE | | ANSWER |
|------|---|--------|
| 1. | _____ in | PLINCE |
| 2. | Full of enjoyment | SLEZFTU |
| 3. | Type of faith | YYLLOAT |
| 4. | Regarded with reverence | SCARDE |

**CLUE:** *Natural* _____

BONUS

**How to play** Complete the crossword puzzle by looking at the clues and unscrambling the answers. When the puzzle is complete, unscramble the circled letters to solve the BONUS.

# PUZZLE

# #87

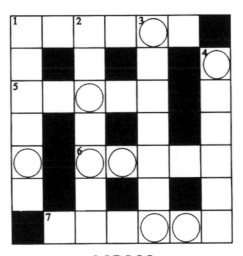

## JUMBLE CROSSWORDS™

### ACROSS

| CLUE | ANSWER |
|------|--------|
| 1. Singer *Anderson* | RILEAU |
| 5. Danger | LIPRE |
| 6. Outspoken | CLAVO |
| 7. Overlayed with metal | DATELP |

### DOWN

| CLUE | ANSWER |
|------|--------|
| 1. Cut off | PDLEOP |
| 2. Fall apart | VANRULE |
| 3. Not legally permitted | TILILIC |
| 4. Sent for delivery | ADIMEL |

**CLUE:** Longer play or higher pay

**BONUS**

**How to play** Complete the crossword puzzle by looking at the clues and unscrambling the answers. When the puzzle is complete, unscramble the circled letters to solve the BONUS.

# #88

## JUMBLE CROSSWORDS™

**ACROSS**

| CLUE | | ANSWER |
|---|---|---|
| 1. | Recognition | TEIRCD |
| 5. | Dice for example | SCEBU |
| 6. | Tablet | TESLA |
| 7. | Method | YESSMT |

**DOWN**

| CLUE | | ANSWER |
|---|---|---|
| 1. | _____ clock | KCCOUO |
| 2. | Official offices | SMYBASE |
| 3. | Immediate | TTANISN |
| 4. | Wax _____ | UUMSME |

**CLUE:** "This" is it

**BONUS**
2 WORDS

○○○○○   ○○○○

**How to play** Complete the crossword puzzle by looking at the clues and unscrambling the answers. When the puzzle is complete, unscramble the circled letters to solve the BONUS.

# JUMBLE CROSSWORDS™

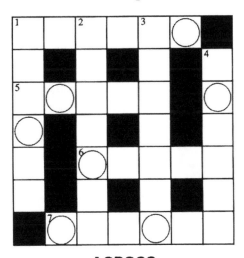

## ACROSS

| CLUE | ANSWER |
|------|--------|
| 1. Respect | GEMAOH |
| 5. Photographer *Bachman* | NKEAR |
| 6. "Kramer" | MOOSC |
| 7. Learned by experience | SLOESN |

## DOWN

| CLUE | ANSWER |
|------|--------|
| 1. Walking in the woods | HNIIGK |
| 2. Extraordinary event | REALMCI |
| 3. Coming into being | GSNIEES |
| 4. The north side | NUWOPT |

**CLUE:** Important

**BONUS**

How to play — Complete the crossword puzzle by looking at the clues and unscrambling the answers. When the puzzle is complete, unscramble the circled letters to solve the BONUS.

# #90

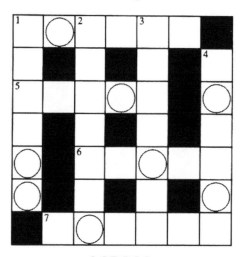

## JUMBLE CROSSWORDS™

### ACROSS

| CLUE | ANSWER |
|------|--------|
| 1. *Park* _____ | E E U N V A |
| 5. Chords, strings | S C E A L |
| 6. Speak | E T R O A |
| 7. Guard, soldier | T Y R N E S |

### DOWN

| CLUE | ANSWER |
|------|--------|
| 1. In poor health | A G N I L I |
| 2. Surround | C L E N E O S |
| 3. A new business | T T U A P R S |
| 4. 3+34+47+17-12+1= | E Y T I N N |

**CLUE:** No

BONUS

How to play   Complete the crossword puzzle by looking at the clues and unscrambling the answers. When the puzzle is complete, unscramble the circled letters to solve the BONUS.

 #91

# JUMBLE CROSSWORDS™

## ACROSS

| CLUE | ANSWER |
|------|--------|
| 1. Collect | R A G E H T |
| 5. A body movement | G U H R S |
| 6. Optical counterpart | A I M G E |
| 7. Sticky substance | T E E M N C |

## DOWN

| CLUE | ANSWER |
|------|--------|
| 1. Talk, rumor | S P I G S O |
| 2. Destructive insect | T T E E I M R |
| 3. Etch letters | V G N E E R A |
| 4. Turmoil | S T U N E R |

CLUE: *David L. Hoyt*

BONUS ○○○○○○○○○

**How to play** Complete the crossword puzzle by looking at the clues and unscrambling the answers. When the puzzle is complete, unscramble the circled letters to solve the BONUS.

# #92

# JUMBLE CROSSWORDS™

## ACROSS

| CLUE | ANSWER |
|------|--------|
| 1. One way to advertise | TEPSRO |
| 5. Monotonous sound | RNOED |
| 6. Tropical fruit | GAMON |
| 7. Type of jewelry | TALKEN |

## DOWN

| CLUE | ANSWER |
|------|--------|
| 1. Platform | DIMOPU |
| 2. "Frosty" | ONNAWSM |
| 3. The _____ Flame | NEELTAR |
| 4. An attempt | REFTOF |

**CLUE:** *Fast _____*

## BONUS ◯◯◯◯◯◯◯

**How to play**  Complete the crossword puzzle by looking at the clues and unscrambling the answers. When the puzzle is complete, unscramble the circled letters to solve the BONUS.

# #93

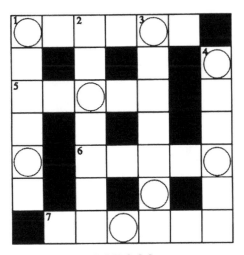

**JUMBLE CROSSWORDS**

## ACROSS

| CLUE | | ANSWER |
|---|---|---|
| 1. | Italian city | SLANPE |
| 5. | Language | GONIL |
| 6. | _____ acid | NOIMA |
| 7. | Mixes | BDELNS |

## DOWN

| CLUE | | ANSWER |
|---|---|---|
| 1. | Singer *Willie* | NNOESL |
| 2. | _____ machine | BANLLIP |
| 3. | Grand Canyon producer | SNOOREI |
| 4. | Stockings | NSNLOY |

**CLUE:** A type of basketball game or conversation

**BONUS**
3 WORDS

How to play — Complete the crossword puzzle by looking at the clues and unscrambling the answers. When the puzzle is complete, unscramble the circled letters to solve the BONUS.

# JUMBLE CROSSWORDS™

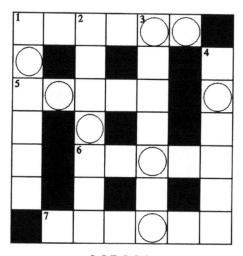

## ACROSS

| CLUE | ANSWER |
|---|---|
| 1. Conjecture | RTYOEH |
| 5. Reason for shoeshine | UFSFC |
| 6. Empty, vacant | IEANN |
| 7. Communication attempt | SEECAN |

## DOWN

| CLUE | ANSWER |
|---|---|
| 1. Thrown | STEODS |
| 2. Hard to find | LVEEIUS |
| 3. Recurring verse, phrase | FERNIAR |
| 4. Unit of electric current | PRAMEE |

**CLUE:** RADAR and MASH

BONUS

How to play  Complete the crossword puzzle by looking at the clues and unscrambling the answers. When the puzzle is complete, unscramble the circled letters to solve the BONUS.

# #95

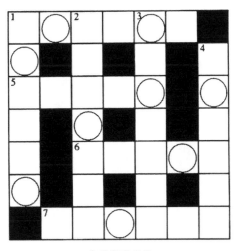

**JUMBLE CROSSWORDS**

## ACROSS

| CLUE | ANSWER |
|------|--------|
| 1. Form of high praise | EGOYUL |
| 5. _____ *Woods* | GRITE |
| 6. You can *make* one | FEORF |
| 7. *Yes* _____ | DEINDE |

## DOWN

| CLUE | ANSWER |
|------|--------|
| 1. Being | TNIYET |
| 2. "Foghorn's" last name | ROGHELN |
| 3. Tall mammal | AFRIGEF |
| 4. *William* or *Robert* | CRANDO |

**CLUE:** One type has four legs, another has four wheels

BONUS

**How to play** Complete the crossword puzzle by looking at the clues and unscrambling the answers. When the puzzle is complete, unscramble the circled letters to solve the BONUS.

## JUMBLE CROSSWORDS™

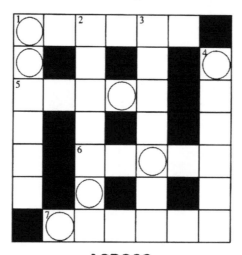

### ACROSS

| CLUE | ANSWER |
|------|--------|
| 1. New Jersey city | R N W E A K |
| 5. *Elliott's* first name | H I C S R |
| 6. Exclusive of anyone | E N L O A |
| 7. Me and them to you | S T O E H R |

### DOWN

| CLUE | ANSWER |
|------|--------|
| 1. _____ *Kidman* | C L E N O I |
| 2. Give adequate reason | W A N T R R A |
| 3. Renew | R R T S E E O |
| 4. Stefanie's last name | O W P E S R |

**CLUE:** I would give you mine, if you asked me for it

**BONUS**

How to play — Complete the crossword puzzle by looking at the clues and unscrambling the answers. When the puzzle is complete, unscramble the circled letters to solve the BONUS.

# JUMBLE CROSSWORDS™

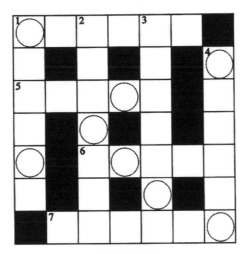

## ACROSS

| CLUE | ANSWER |
|---|---|
| 1. Affected by supply | MEADDN |
| 5. *Vantage* _____ | TIPNO |
| 6. Light source | COTHR |
| 7. This is made of bone | TELRAN |

## DOWN

| CLUE | ANSWER |
|---|---|
| 1. Place reliance | DDNEEP |
| 2. Wet | NOMEITS |
| 3. _____ *resources* | NLAARUT |
| 4. Rodent family member | PREHOG |

**CLUE:** You must be male to be one

**BONUS**

**How to play**  Complete the crossword puzzle by looking at the clues and unscrambling the answers. When the puzzle is complete, unscramble the circled letters to solve the BONUS.

# #98

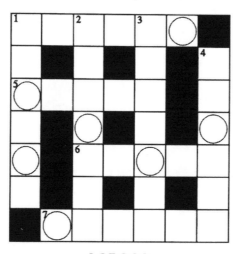

## JUMBLE CROSSWORDS™

### ACROSS

| CLUE | ANSWER |
|------|--------|
| 1. Distance | TNEHGL |
| 5. U.S. port city | AATPM |
| 6. Long-_____ | GAREN |
| 7. Around the longest | STODLE |

### DOWN

| CLUE | ANSWER |
|------|--------|
| 1. Medicinal liquid | OOINTL |
| 2. "V" for example | NMAREUL |
| 3. Beginner | ARTENIE |
| 4. Assimilate mentally | STEDGI |

**CLUE:** Busy

**BONUS**
3 WORDS

**How to play**  Complete the crossword puzzle by looking at the clues and unscrambling the answers. When the puzzle is complete, unscramble the circled letters to solve the BONUS.

# #99

## JUMBLE CROSSWORDS™

### ACROSS

| CLUE | ANSWER |
|------|--------|
| 1. Open | PAWRNU |
| 5. A single step | RASTI |
| 6. From this source | NCHEE |
| 7. Cue | MRTOPP |

### DOWN

| CLUE | ANSWER |
|------|--------|
| 1. Not spoken | DANSUI |
| 2. Winter _____ | HATWREE |
| 3. "Laser" for example | CAMYNOR |
| 4. "_____ Night" | TISNEL |

CLUE: "My wish to you...Happy _____" D.L.H.

BONUS

How to play — Complete the crossword puzzle by looking at the clues and unscrambling the answers. When the puzzle is complete, unscramble the circled letters to solve the BONUS.

# JUMBLE CROSSWORDS™

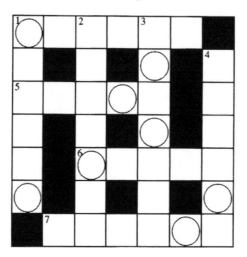

## ACROSS

| CLUE | | ANSWER |
|------|---|--------|
| 1. | Small rounded body | TPEELL |
| 5. | _____ *button* | NCPIA |
| 6. | Filled, covered | SHAWA |
| 7. | A keyboard key | EEELTD |

## DOWN

| CLUE | | ANSWER |
|------|---|--------|
| 1. | Students | SLIPPU |
| 2. | Ancestry | GAINEEL |
| 3. | Distinct social unit | CAEVLEN |
| 4. | "Gloria's" father | HARICE |

**CLUE:** Sustained, severe decline

BONUS

**How to play**  Complete the crossword puzzle by looking at the clues and unscrambling the answers. When the puzzle is complete, unscramble the circled letters to solve the BONUS.

101

# PUZZLE

# #101

## JUMBLE CROSSWORDS™

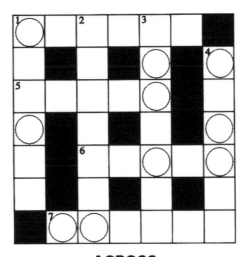

### ACROSS

| CLUE | ANSWER |
|------|--------|
| 1. Prevent by command | BIFDOR |
| 5. B-_____ | EMIOV |
| 6. Type of banquet | STORA |
| 7. Car part | NREFDE |

### DOWN

| CLUE | ANSWER |
|------|--------|
| 1. Widely known | SFUAOM |
| 2. Invert | VEEESRR |
| 3. An island country | DILENCA |
| 4. Type of depression | RATREC |

**CLUE:** A type of conversation you can't have on the telephone

**BONUS**
3 WORDS

**How to play** Complete the crossword puzzle by looking at the clues and unscrambling the answers. When the puzzle is complete, unscramble the circled letters to solve the BONUS.

# #102

## JUMBLE CROSSWORDS™

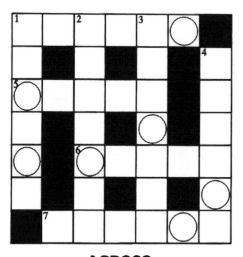

### ACROSS

| CLUE | | ANSWER |
|------|--|--------|
| 1. | Prosper | R I T E H V |
| 5. | To come into | C R I N U |
| 6. | Spin | L T R W I |
| 7. | A quick body movement | N F H C I L |

### DOWN

| CLUE | | ANSWER |
|------|--|--------|
| 1. | Intricate, deceitful | K I T C R Y |
| 2. | A performance | T R C I E L A |
| 3. | A particular form | S N E R V I O |
| 4. | General condition | L H H A T E |

**CLUE:** Their location may determine their price

## BONUS

**How to play** Complete the crossword puzzle by looking at the clues and unscrambling the answers. When the puzzle is complete, unscramble the circled letters to solve the BONUS.

# JUMBLE® CROSSWORDS™

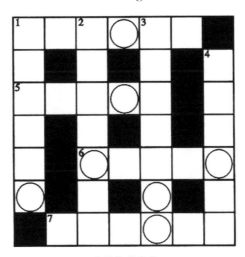

## ACROSS

| CLUE | ANSWER |
|------|--------|
| 1. A *J.T.* and *O.N.J.* movie | SEEGAR |
| 5. Grown in the ground | STEBE |
| 6. A man's name | SACIA |
| 7. Plan | DEAANG |

## DOWN

| CLUE | ANSWER |
|------|--------|
| 1. A type of drinking glass | TEBLOG |
| 2. When the sun goes down | GEENVIN |
| 3. Uphold | SSTNAIU |
| 4. One of the "Bunch" | CIMRAA |

**CLUE:** Found at the bottom of the sea

**BONUS**

**How to play** Complete the crossword puzzle by looking at the clues and unscrambling the answers. When the puzzle is complete, unscramble the circled letters to solve the BONUS.

# JUMBLE CROSSWORDS™

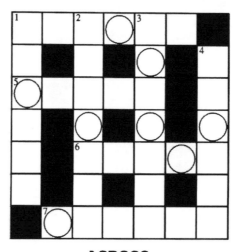

## ACROSS

| CLUE | | ANSWER |
|------|---|--------|
| 1. | Something strange | YDTDIO |
| 5. | Irritation or trouble | NROTH |
| 6. | A famous philosopher | TOPLA |
| 7. | Important | TURNGE |

## DOWN

| CLUE | | ANSWER |
|------|---|--------|
| 1. | Clothes | FTOTUI |
| 2. | An eye _____ | PORDREP |
| 3. | Capacity, weight | GONNTEA |
| 4. | Grow | STUORP |

**CLUE:** A type of output

BONUS

How to play   Complete the crossword puzzle by looking at the clues and unscrambling the answers. When the puzzle is complete, unscramble the circled letters to solve the BONUS.

# #105

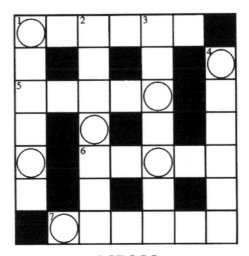

**JUMBLE CROSSWORDS™**

## ACROSS

| CLUE | ANSWER |
|---|---|
| 1. Small in degree | HISTLG |
| 5. *Pony, sleigh* or *bike* | SRIED |
| 6. You can *get caught* at this | GILYN |
| 7. By means of this | BEERHY |

## DOWN

| CLUE | ANSWER |
|---|---|
| 1. To be frugal | SPIRCM |
| 2. Yield to a desire | GELNIDU |
| 3. Antagonistic | OLISTHE |
| 4. Model, actress | GIGYWT |

**CLUE:** A land connector

**BONUS** ○○○○○○○

How to play  Complete the crossword puzzle by looking at the clues and unscrambling the answers. When the puzzle is complete, unscramble the circled letters to solve the BONUS.

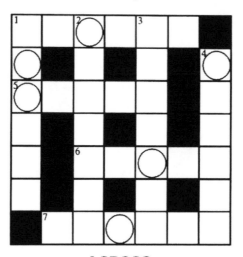

## JUMBLE CROSSWORDS™

### ACROSS

| CLUE | ANSWER |
|------|--------|
| 1. Fraternity status | GEDELP |
| 5. A *Monkee* | TREEP |
| 6. A decree | CEITD |
| 7. To fasten | THEERT |

### DOWN

| CLUE | ANSWER |
|------|--------|
| 1. A rapidly growing tree | POLARP |
| 2. Utmost | TEEERMX |
| 3. Ornamental additive | SIGNRAH |
| 4. An alloy containing tin | TWEERP |

**CLUE:** *Chicken* is one variety of this

**BONUS** ◯◯◯◯◯◯

How to play — Complete the crossword puzzle by looking at the clues and unscrambling the answers. When the puzzle is complete, unscramble the circled letters to solve the BONUS.

# #107

## JUMBLE CROSSWORDS™

### ACROSS

| CLUE | ANSWER |
|------|--------|
| 1. Country capital | WOTAAT |
| 5. Majestic | GLERA |
| 6. Fictional dwarf | LTLOR |
| 7. Weird | PRECYE |

### DOWN

| CLUE | ANSWER |
|------|--------|
| 1. Surging movement | RONSUH |
| 2. Firmer | GITETHR |
| 3. *Mat* greeting | MEWOLCE |
| 4. Actually | LAREYL |

**CLUE:** This is home to approx. 10 million people

**BONUS** ◯◯◯◯◯◯◯◯

**How to play** Complete the crossword puzzle by looking at the clues and unscrambling the answers. When the puzzle is complete, unscramble the circled letters to solve the BONUS.

# PUZZLE

# #108

# JUMBLE CROSSWORDS™

## ACROSS

| CLUE | ANSWER |
|------|--------|
| 1. _____ gun | EPATSL |
| 5. A U.S. state | AOIHD |
| 6. Bumbling | PINET |
| 7. Together | OSUNIN |

## DOWN

| CLUE | ANSWER |
|------|--------|
| 1. Seasoned | DECPIS |
| 2. _____ horse | NAAAIRB |
| 3. Large feline | SLINSOE |
| 4. Container | NCOATR |

**CLUE:** *"I need these...You may or may not"*

BONUS ○○○○○○○○

How to play — Complete the crossword puzzle by looking at the clues and unscrambling the answers. When the puzzle is complete, unscramble the circled letters to solve the BONUS.

109

# JUMBLE CROSSWORDS™

## ACROSS

| CLUE | ANSWER |
|---|---|
| 1. Crack, break | EEDDOC |
| 5. Souvenir | CRIEL |
| 6. Glowing fragment | BRMEE |
| 7. Font style | CITIAL |

## DOWN

| CLUE | ANSWER |
|---|---|
| 1. Force | RUDSES |
| 2. Cluster | TLCLOCE |
| 3. Degree of loudness | BIDEELC |
| 4. _____ acid | CINIRT |

**CLUE:** Event

BONUS ◯◯◯◯◯◯◯◯◯◯

**How to play** Complete the crossword puzzle by looking at the clues and unscrambling the answers. When the puzzle is complete, unscramble the circled letters to solve the BONUS.

# JUMBLE CROSSWORDS™

## ACROSS

| CLUE | ANSWER |
|---|---|
| 1. Historical nemesis | U U S T R B |
| 5. Luminous | D I L C U |
| 6. Metrical language | S R E E V |
| 7. Soldiers | S P O R T O |

## DOWN

| CLUE | ANSWER |
|---|---|
| 1. Song | D B A L A L |
| 2. Expose | O N E C U R V |
| 3. Experience | E N D U G O R |
| 4. Bladed arms | P I E W S R |

**CLUE:** *"I had _____ _____ for breakfast today"*

**BONUS**
2 WORDS
○○○ ○○○○○○

**How to play**  Complete the crossword puzzle by looking at the clues and unscrambling the answers. When the puzzle is complete, unscramble the circled letters to solve the BONUS.

 #111

# JUMBLE CROSSWORDS™

## ACROSS

| CLUE | ANSWER |
|------|--------|
| 1. Former members | MANIUL |
| 5. A type of fish | BREMA |
| 6. Driving _____ | NRAEG |
| 7. Dwelling style | TCEALH |

## DOWN

| CLUE | ANSWER |
|------|--------|
| 1. A U.S. city | BNYAAL |
| 2. Find | AERNUHT |
| 3. Small | LMONIAN |
| 4. Magnitude | NTTXEE |

**CLUE:** *"If someone can solve this whole puzzle in under 60 seconds, and e-mail me to tell me about it at DLHoyt@aol.com, I will donate some money to a good cause today."* D.L.H

**BONUS**
2 WORDS

**How to play** Complete the crossword puzzle by looking at the clues and unscrambling the answers. When the puzzle is complete, unscramble the circled letters to solve the BONUS.

# #112

## JUMBLE CROSSWORDS™

### ACROSS

| CLUE | | ANSWER |
|------|--|--------|
| 1. | Calm | L C D I A P |
| 5. | *Kemp* or *Kennedy* | N S W A H |
| 6. | Records | E O S N T |
| 7. | Workplace | O D I S T U |

### DOWN

| CLUE | | ANSWER |
|------|--|--------|
| 1. | Harass | E E P R T S |
| 2. | Contrary | A A T S I N G |
| 3. | Set off | T I D I G E N |
| 4. | Complete failure | O C A F I S |

**CLUE:** Valid

**BONUS**

How to play — Complete the crossword puzzle by looking at the clues and unscrambling the answers. When the puzzle is complete, unscramble the circled letters to solve the BONUS.

# #113

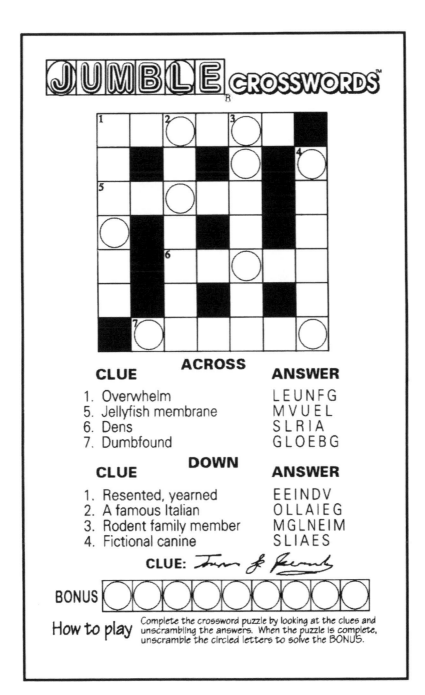

## JUMBLE CROSSWORDS™

### ACROSS

| CLUE | ANSWER |
|------|--------|
| 1. Overwhelm | LEUNFG |
| 5. Jellyfish membrane | MVUEL |
| 6. Dens | SLRIA |
| 7. Dumbfound | GLOEBG |

### DOWN

| CLUE | ANSWER |
|------|--------|
| 1. Resented, yearned | EEINDV |
| 2. A famous Italian | OLLAIEG |
| 3. Rodent family member | MGLNEIM |
| 4. Fictional canine | SLIAES |

CLUE:

BONUS

How to play — Complete the crossword puzzle by looking at the clues and unscrambling the answers. When the puzzle is complete, unscramble the circled letters to solve the BONUS.

# JUMBLE CROSSWORDS™

## ACROSS

| CLUE | ANSWER |
|------|--------|
| 1. _____ puzzle | GJIAWS |
| 5. Things | FUSTF |
| 6. Containers | XOBSE |
| 7. Seller | REDONV |

## DOWN

| CLUE | ANSWER |
|------|--------|
| 1. Acting *Mazzello* | JHPOES |
| 2. Complain | MURGELB |
| 3. Attached | FIDEXAF |
| 4. _____ salad | SARAEC |

**CLUE:** Place together

BONUS

**How to play** Complete the crossword puzzle by looking at the clues and unscrambling the answers. When the puzzle is complete, unscramble the circled letters to solve the BONUS.

#115

# JUMBLE CROSSWORDS™

## ACROSS

| CLUE | ANSWER |
|---|---|
| 1. Cutting machine | WIJASG |
| 5. Pack | UTFSF |
| 6. Fights | XSEOB |
| 7. Peddler | NDVOER |

## DOWN

| CLUE | ANSWER |
|---|---|
| 1. A man's name | SHOPEJ |
| 2. Mutter | MELBURG |
| 3. Fastened | FIADEXF |
| 4. Augustus _____ | SRAEAC |

**CLUE:** You can feel this, but you can't touch it

**BONUS**
2 WORDS

○○○○  ○○

How to play — Complete the crossword puzzle by looking at the clues and unscrambling the answers. When the puzzle is complete, unscramble the circled letters to solve the BONUS.

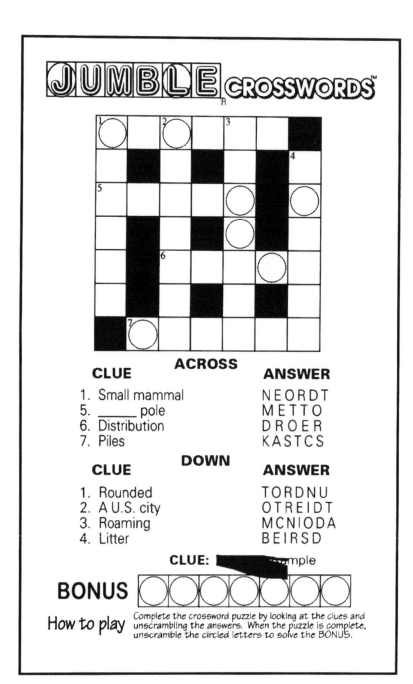

# JUMBLE CROSSWORDS™

## ACROSS

| CLUE | ANSWER |
|------|--------|
| 1. Small mammal | N E O R D T |
| 5. _____ pole | M E T T O |
| 6. Distribution | D R O E R |
| 7. Piles | K A S T C S |

## DOWN

| CLUE | ANSWER |
|------|--------|
| 1. Rounded | T O R D N U |
| 2. A U.S. city | O T R E I D T |
| 3. Roaming | M C N I O D A |
| 4. Litter | B E I R S D |

CLUE: ▨▨ mple

BONUS ○○○○○○○

How to play  Complete the crossword puzzle by looking at the clues and
unscrambling the answers. When the puzzle is complete,
unscramble the circled letters to solve the BONUS.

 #117

# JUMBLE CROSSWORDS™

**ACROSS**

| CLUE | ANSWER |
|---|---|
| 1. With pleasure | LLDYAG |
| 5. Many times | NOETF |
| 6. Send | MRIET |
| 7. Greek _____ | DSINOA |

**DOWN**

| CLUE | ANSWER |
|---|---|
| 1. Store owner | CRGREO |
| 2. Dressed | TDAITER |
| 3. Football position | NLAIMEN |
| 4. Free | SGIRTA |

**CLUE:** Archibald Leach's stage name

BONUS
2 WORDS

How to play — Complete the crossword puzzle by looking at the clues and unscrambling the answers. When the puzzle is complete, unscramble the circled letters to solve the BONUS.

JUMBLE CROSSWORDS™

**ACROSS**

| CLUE | ANSWER |
|------|--------|
| 1. Lasso | R L I A A T |
| 5. Performing | G D N I O |
| 6. Money | D A R E B |
| 7. Wrap | T S A W E H |

**DOWN**

| CLUE | ANSWER |
|------|--------|
| 1. Inns | D O L S E G |
| 2. Multicolored array | B A R O I N W |
| 3. Increase | A E M T N G U |
| 4. Head, brain | D O L O N E |

**CLUE:** *"I was _____ when I made this puzzle"*

BONUS  ◯◯◯◯◯◯◯◯

How to play  Complete the crossword puzzle by looking at the clues and unscrambling the answers. When the puzzle is complete, unscramble the circled letters to solve the BONUS.

# JUMBLE CROSSWORDS™

## ACROSS

| CLUE | ANSWER |
|---|---|
| 1. Spread | LWPARS |
| 5. Speed | TPOME |
| 6. Asian monarchy | PLNAE |
| 7. European polecat | RFEETR |

## DOWN

| CLUE | ANSWER |
|---|---|
| 1. Sixth of nine | TASRNU |
| 2. _____ languages | MORENAC |
| 3. Lie | OPHREPW |
| 4. Small village | MAHTEL |

**BONUS**
2 WORDS  **CLUE:** This was patented on Jan. 20, 1885

How to play   Complete the crossword puzzle by looking at the clues and unscrambling the answers. When the puzzle is complete, unscramble the circled letters to solve the BONUS.

# #120

## JUMBLE CROSSWORDS™

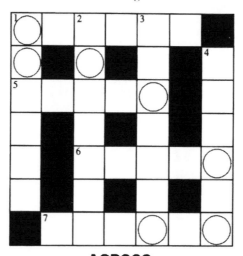

### ACROSS

| CLUE | ANSWER |
|------|--------|
| 1. *1, 5, 6 or 7* _____ | SARSOC |
| 5. Pester, annoy | TSEEA |
| 6. Fatigued | RDTIE |
| 7. Switched | DDTEAR |

### DOWN

| CLUE | ANSWER |
|------|--------|
| 1. Song | MATENH |
| 2. *Nuclear* _____ | RROTAEC |
| 3. Cut, cropped | DSEHRAE |
| 4. Touched down | NALDDE |

**CLUE:** A reason to turn around

**BONUS**
2 WORDS

How to play — Complete the crossword puzzle by looking at the clues and unscrambling the answers. When the puzzle is complete, unscramble the circled letters to solve the BONUS.

121

# #121

## JUMBLE CROSSWORDS™

### ACROSS

| CLUE | | ANSWER |
|------|---|--------|
| 1. | Constraint | S D U E R S |
| 5. | Spinning machine | A E T H L |
| 6. | Olive family member | C L I A L |
| 7. | Followed | T A R D C E |

### DOWN

| CLUE | | ANSWER |
|------|---|--------|
| 1. | Money | L O D R A L |
| 2. | American pit viper | A R R L T E T |
| 3. | Defeat decisively | L H S E C A L |
| 4. | Cut | C M N I D E |

**CLUE:** Position

BONUS ◯◯◯◯◯◯◯◯◯

How to play   Complete the crossword puzzle by looking at the clues and unscrambling the answers. When the puzzle is complete, unscramble the circled letters to solve the BONUS.

# PUZZLE

# #122

## JUMBLE CROSSWORDS™

### ACROSS

| CLUE | ANSWER |
|------|--------|
| 1. Hurt | N F E F D O |
| 5. _____ Leigh | J E T N A |
| 6. Narrow body of water | T I E L N |
| 7. Concurred | E A R D E G |

### DOWN

| CLUE | ANSWER |
|------|--------|
| 1. Argue against | B C J T E O |
| 2. A sport | C N F G I E N |
| 3. _____ Wood | N E I A T L A |
| 4. Guaranteed benefits | D V E E T S |

**CLUE:** Drop

**BONUS** ○○○○○○○○

How to play — Complete the crossword puzzle by looking at the clues and unscrambling the answers. When the puzzle is complete, unscramble the circled letters to solve the BONUS.

#123

JUMBLE CROSSWORDS™

**ACROSS**

| CLUE | ANSWER |
|------|--------|
| 1. A carnivorous mammal | SAWLEE |
| 5. Lodging | TLEOM |
| 6. Prank | RPCEA |
| 7. Thin layer | EEERNV |

**DOWN**

| CLUE | ANSWER |
|------|--------|
| 1. Australian marsupial | ATMOBW |
| 2. Piece | TRACIEL |
| 3. ⬭ | PILLEES |
| 4. _____ movie | RRROOH |

CLUE: "The next bonus will reference this bonus," for example

**BONUS** ◯◯◯◯◯◯◯

**How to play** Complete the crossword puzzle by looking at the clues and unscrambling the answers. When the puzzle is complete, unscramble the circled letters to solve the BONUS.

124

# #124

## JUMBLE CROSSWORDS™

### ACROSS

| CLUE | ANSWER |
|------|--------|
| 1. Furnace feeder | R S E T K O |
| 5. Nocturnal mammal | N A E H Y |
| 6. Refashion | A R T E L |
| 7. Bumper | D E E N R F |

### DOWN

| CLUE | ANSWER |
|------|--------|
| 1. Summer _____ | H S L O C O |
| 2. Run | R E P T E A O |
| 3. Constituted | C A N E D E T |
| 4. Holder | R R E E B A |

**CLUE:** The previous bonus answer was "preview"

BONUS ○○○○○○○○○

**How to play** Complete the crossword puzzle by looking at the clues and unscrambling the answers. When the puzzle is complete, unscramble the circled letters to solve the BONUS.

# JUMBLE CROSSWORDS™

## ACROSS

| CLUE | ANSWER |
|------|--------|
| 1. Shelter | FRGUEE |
| 5. Cut | CINEM |
| 6. Leader | RLEUR |
| 7. Enough | NELYTP |

## DOWN

| CLUE | ANSWER |
|------|--------|
| 1. Distant | OEERTM |
| 2. _____ director | LFAUREN |
| 3. Mischievous gnome | MERGNIL |
| 4. Exuberant | EYHTRA |

**BONUS** 3 WORDS    **CLUE:** Again and again

How to play — Complete the crossword puzzle by looking at the clues and unscrambling the answers. When the puzzle is complete, unscramble the circled letters to solve the BONUS.

# #126

## JUMBLE CROSSWORDS™

### ACROSS

| CLUE | ANSWER |
|------|--------|
| 1. Gather | RMEUTS |
| 5. Holding device | PALSC |
| 6. Pulled | ODWET |
| 7. Long vehicle | RSHEEA |

### DOWN

| CLUE | ANSWER |
|------|--------|
| 1. Taunted | CODMEK |
| 2. A large city | ETSLETA |
| 3. Enable | WOMERPE |
| 4. An instrument | DFDIEL |

**CLUE:** John Wayne's father's profession

BONUS ◯◯◯◯◯◯◯◯◯◯

**How to play** Complete the crossword puzzle by looking at the clues and unscrambling the answers. When the puzzle is complete, unscramble the circled letters to solve the BONUS.

# #127

## JUMBLE CROSSWORDS™

### ACROSS

| CLUE | ANSWER |
|------|--------|
| 1. Available money | B D U T G E |
| 5. Comic strip frame | P L E N A |
| 6. Advice | I T U N P |
| 7. *Wall* _____ | S E R T T E |

### DOWN

| CLUE | ANSWER |
|------|--------|
| 1. Hit | P P D E B O |
| 2. A type of doctor | T E N D S I T |
| 3. Surpass | L E C E S P I |
| 4. A group of seven | T T E E P S |

**CLUE:** Crazy

**BONUS** ○○○○○○○○○

**How to play** Complete the crossword puzzle by looking at the clues and unscrambling the answers. When the puzzle is complete, unscramble the circled letters to solve the BONUS.

# MORE JUMBLE® CROSSWORDS

## MASTER PUZZLES

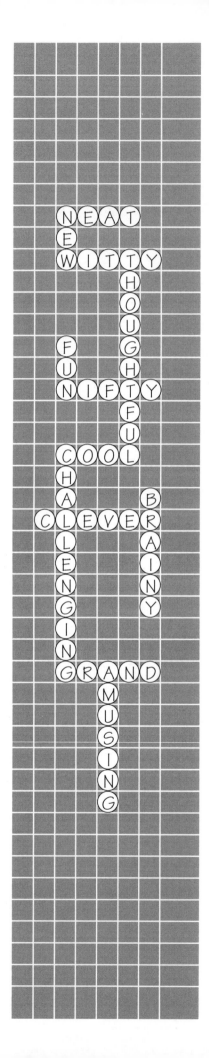

# PUZZLE

# #128

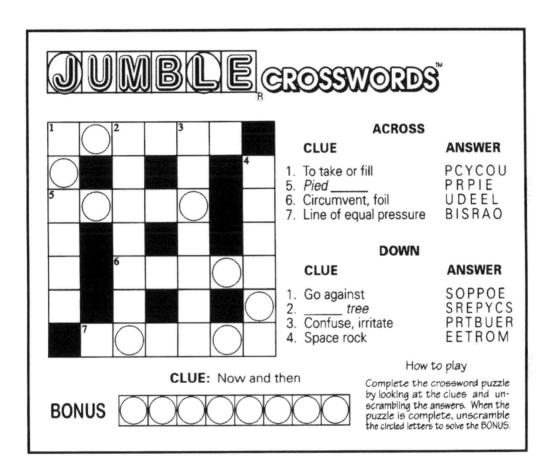

# JUMBLE CROSSWORDS™

**ACROSS**

| CLUE | ANSWER |
|---|---|
| 1. To take or fill | PCYCOU |
| 5. *Pied* _____ | PRPIE |
| 6. Circumvent, foil | UDEEL |
| 7. Line of equal pressure | BISRAO |

**DOWN**

| CLUE | ANSWER |
|---|---|
| 1. Go against | SOPPOE |
| 2. _____ *tree* | SREPYCS |
| 3. Confuse, irritate | PRTBUER |
| 4. Space rock | EETROM |

**CLUE:** Now and then

**BONUS**

How to play

Complete the crossword puzzle by looking at the clues and unscrambling the answers. When the puzzle is complete, unscramble the circled letters to solve the BONUS.

# #129

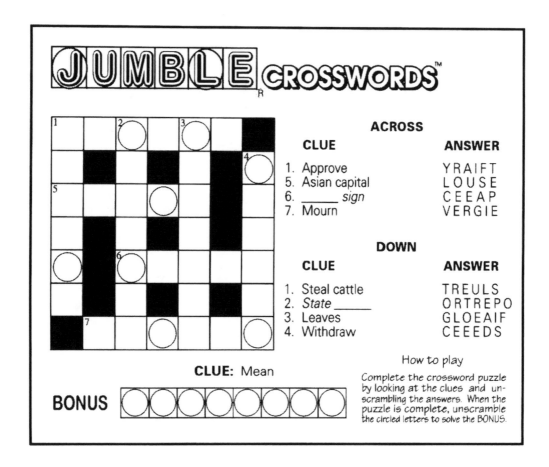

## JUMBLE CROSSWORDS™

### ACROSS

| CLUE | ANSWER |
|------|--------|
| 1. Approve | YRAIFT |
| 5. Asian capital | LOUSE |
| 6. _____ sign | CEEAP |
| 7. Mourn | VERGIE |

### DOWN

| CLUE | ANSWER |
|------|--------|
| 1. Steal cattle | TREULS |
| 2. State _____ | ORTREPO |
| 3. Leaves | GLOEAIF |
| 4. Withdraw | CEEEDS |

#### How to play

Complete the crossword puzzle by looking at the clues and unscrambling the answers. When the puzzle is complete, unscramble the circled letters to solve the BONUS.

**CLUE:** Mean

**BONUS**

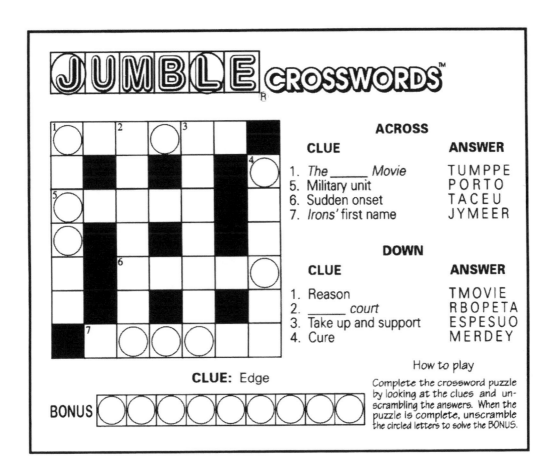

# JUMBLE CROSSWORDS™

## ACROSS

| CLUE | ANSWER |
|------|--------|
| 1. *The* _____ *Movie* | TUMPPE |
| 5. Military unit | PORTO |
| 6. Sudden onset | TACEU |
| 7. *Irons'* first name | JYMEER |

## DOWN

| CLUE | ANSWER |
|------|--------|
| 1. Reason | TMOVIE |
| 2. _____ *court* | RBOPETA |
| 3. Take up and support | ESPESUO |
| 4. Cure | MERDEY |

How to play

Complete the crossword puzzle by looking at the clues and unscrambling the answers. When the puzzle is complete, unscramble the circled letters to solve the BONUS.

**CLUE:** Edge

BONUS

# JUMBLE CROSSWORDS™

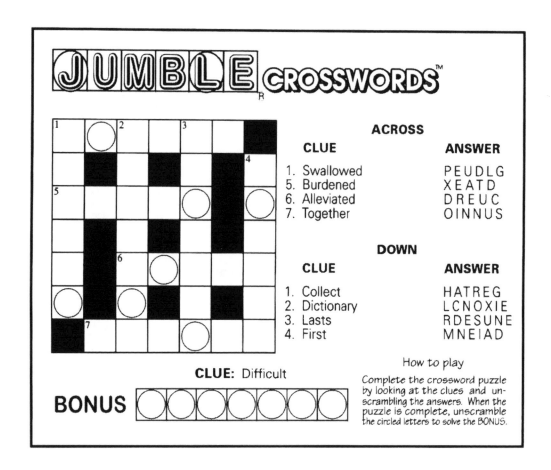

**ACROSS**

| CLUE | ANSWER |
|------|--------|
| 1. Swallowed | PEUDLG |
| 5. Burdened | XEATD |
| 6. Alleviated | DREUC |
| 7. Together | OINNUS |

**DOWN**

| CLUE | ANSWER |
|------|--------|
| 1. Collect | HATREG |
| 2. Dictionary | LCNOXIE |
| 3. Lasts | RDESUNE |
| 4. First | MNEIAD |

**CLUE:** Difficult

BONUS ○○○○○○○

How to play

Complete the crossword puzzle by looking at the clues and unscrambling the answers. When the puzzle is complete, unscramble the circled letters to solve the BONUS.

133

# #132

## JUMBLE CROSSWORDS™

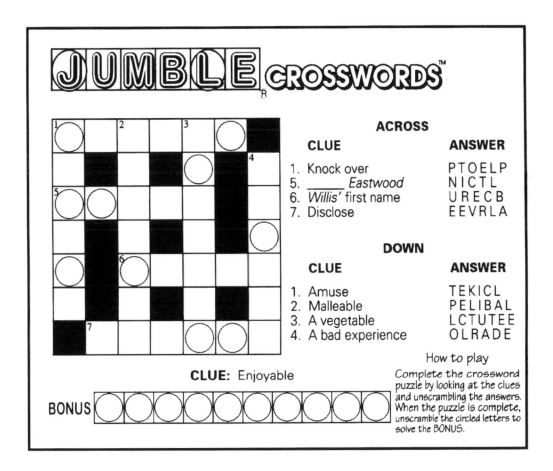

### ACROSS

| CLUE | ANSWER |
|------|--------|
| 1. Knock over | PTOELP |
| 5. _____ Eastwood | NICTL |
| 6. *Willis'* first name | URECB |
| 7. Disclose | EEVRLA |

### DOWN

| CLUE | ANSWER |
|------|--------|
| 1. Amuse | TEKICL |
| 2. Malleable | PELIBAL |
| 3. A vegetable | LCTUTEE |
| 4. A bad experience | OLRADE |

**How to play**

Complete the crossword puzzle by looking at the clues and unscrambling the answers. When the puzzle is complete, unscramble the circled letters to solve the BONUS.

**CLUE:** Enjoyable

BONUS ◯◯◯◯◯◯◯◯◯◯

# JUMBLE CROSSWORDS™

## ACROSS

| CLUE | ANSWER |
|------|--------|
| 1. *Arnold's* last name | RPEAML |
| 5. Estate | AONMR |
| 6. Beyond the usual | TAXRE |
| 7. _____ situation | CYISKT |

## DOWN

| CLUE | ANSWER |
|------|--------|
| 1. Fired up | UDEMPP |
| 2. Extended the most | GONETLS |
| 3. Wandering | CTREAIR |
| 4. Evil reputation | MANYIF |

How to play - Complete the crossword puzzle by looking at the clues and unscrambling the answers. When the puzzle is complete, unscramble the circled letters to solve the BONUS.

CLUE: *I made several of these the other day...I enjoyed every one of them!*

BONUS
3 WORDS

# #134

## JUMBLE CROSSWORDS™

### ACROSS

| CLUE | ANSWER |
|---|---|
| 1. *Rooney's* first name | CIMEYK |
| 5. A grass covering | SORFT |
| 6. A lustrous concretion | LEPAR |
| 7. _____ Circle | TRAICC |

### DOWN

| CLUE | ANSWER |
|---|---|
| 1. *English* _____ | FUNIMF |
| 2. Motorcycle nickname | POCHREP |
| 3. Draw forth | TAXRETC |
| 4. You, me, everyone | LIBCPU |

**CLUE:** Groupings

**BONUS** ○○○○○○○○

### How to play

Complete the crossword puzzle by looking at the clues and unscrambling the answers. When the puzzle is complete, unscramble the circled letters to solve the BONUS.

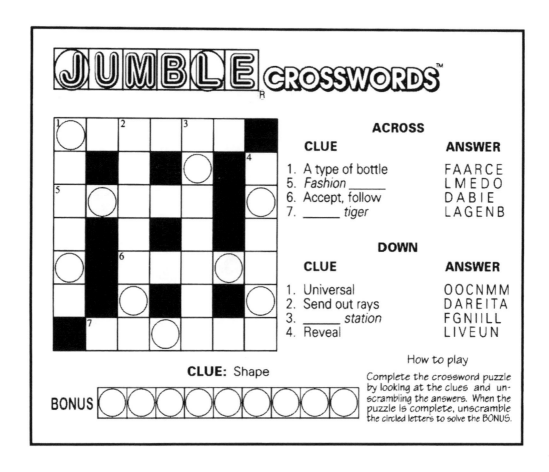

# JUMBLE CROSSWORDS™

## ACROSS

| CLUE | ANSWER |
|------|--------|
| 1. A type of bottle | FAARCE |
| 5. Fashion _____ | LMEDO |
| 6. Accept, follow | DABIE |
| 7. _____ tiger | LAGENB |

## DOWN

| CLUE | ANSWER |
|------|--------|
| 1. Universal | OOCNMM |
| 2. Send out rays | DAREITA |
| 3. _____ station | FGNIILL |
| 4. Reveal | LIVEUN |

**CLUE:** Shape

BONUS ◯◯◯◯◯◯◯◯◯

### How to play

Complete the crossword puzzle by looking at the clues and unscrambling the answers. When the puzzle is complete, unscramble the circled letters to solve the BONUS.

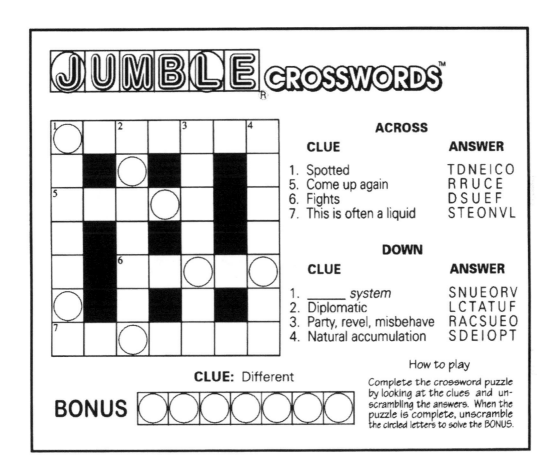

# JUMBLE CROSSWORDS™

## ACROSS

| | CLUE | ANSWER |
|---|---|---|
| 1. | Spotted | TDNEICO |
| 5. | Come up again | RRUCE |
| 6. | Fights | DSUEF |
| 7. | This is often a liquid | STEONVL |

## DOWN

| | CLUE | ANSWER |
|---|---|---|
| 1. | _____ system | SNUEORV |
| 2. | Diplomatic | LCTATUF |
| 3. | Party, revel, misbehave | RACSUEO |
| 4. | Natural accumulation | SDEIOPT |

### How to play

Complete the crossword puzzle by looking at the clues and unscrambling the answers. When the puzzle is complete, unscramble the circled letters to solve the BONUS.

**CLUE:** Different

BONUS

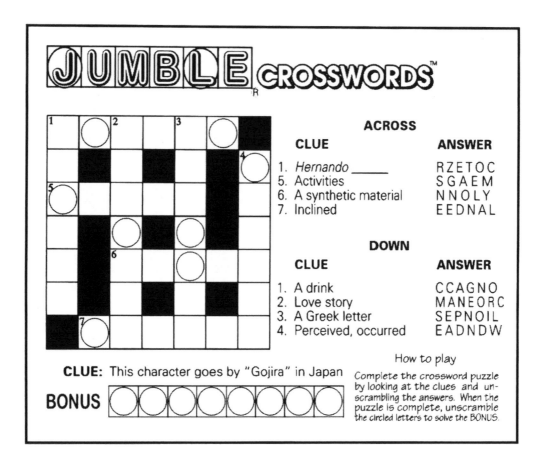

JUMBLE CROSSWORDS™

**ACROSS**

| | CLUE | ANSWER |
|---|---|---|
| 1. | *Hernando _____* | R Z E T O C |
| 5. | Activities | S G A E M |
| 6. | A synthetic material | N N O L Y |
| 7. | Inclined | E E D N A L |

**DOWN**

| | CLUE | ANSWER |
|---|---|---|
| 1. | A drink | C C A G N O |
| 2. | Love story | M A N E O R C |
| 3. | A Greek letter | S E P N O I L |
| 4. | Perceived, occurred | E A D N D W |

**CLUE:** This character goes by "Gojira" in Japan

**BONUS** ◯◯◯◯◯◯◯◯

How to play

Complete the crossword puzzle by looking at the clues and unscrambling the answers. When the puzzle is complete, unscramble the circled letters to solve the BONUS.

#138

# JUMBLE CROSSWORDS™

## ACROSS

| CLUE | ANSWER |
|---|---|
| 1. A colorless gas | M H U E I L |
| 5. Provide a supply of food | C R E A T |
| 6. Understood | G R R E O |
| 7. Dishes | S T E A P L |

## DOWN

| CLUE | ANSWER |
|---|---|
| 1. Crazy | C H I E T C |
| 2. To the side | R A T E A L L |
| 3. Straight up | H I T G R P U |
| 4. Company of singers | S C H U O R |

How to play

Complete the crossword puzzle by looking at the clues and unscrambling the answers. When the puzzle is complete, unscramble the circled letters to solve the BONUS.

CLUE: Maybe

BONUS

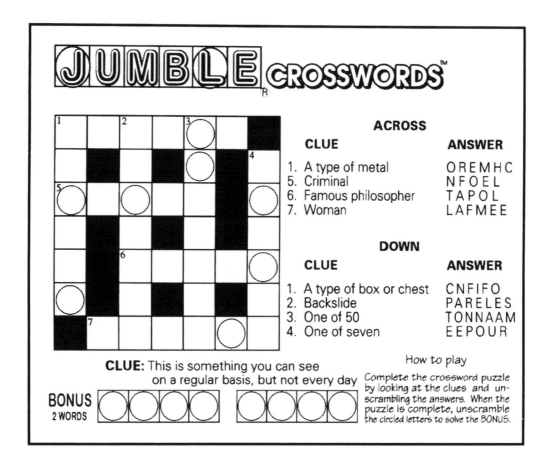

# JUMBLE CROSSWORDS™

## ACROSS

| CLUE | ANSWER |
|------|--------|
| 1. A type of metal | OREMHC |
| 5. Criminal | NFOEL |
| 6. Famous philosopher | TAPOL |
| 7. Woman | LAFMEE |

## DOWN

| CLUE | ANSWER |
|------|--------|
| 1. A type of box or chest | CNFIFO |
| 2. Backslide | PARELES |
| 3. One of 50 | TONNAAM |
| 4. One of seven | EEPOUR |

### How to play

Complete the crossword puzzle by looking at the clues and unscrambling the answers. When the puzzle is complete, unscramble the circled letters to solve the BONUS.

**CLUE:** This is something you can see on a regular basis, but not every day

**BONUS** 2 WORDS

# PUZZLE #140

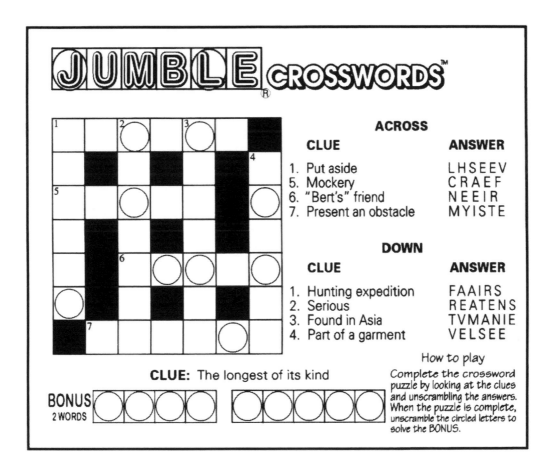

## JUMBLE CROSSWORDS™

### ACROSS

| CLUE | ANSWER |
|------|--------|
| 1. Put aside | LHSEEV |
| 5. Mockery | CRAEF |
| 6. "Bert's" friend | NEEIR |
| 7. Present an obstacle | MYISTE |

### DOWN

| CLUE | ANSWER |
|------|--------|
| 1. Hunting expedition | FAAIRS |
| 2. Serious | REATENS |
| 3. Found in Asia | TVMANIE |
| 4. Part of a garment | VELSEE |

How to play

Complete the crossword puzzle by looking at the clues and unscrambling the answers. When the puzzle is complete, unscramble the circled letters to solve the BONUS.

**CLUE:** The longest of its kind

BONUS
2 WORDS

142

## JUMBLE CROSSWORDS™

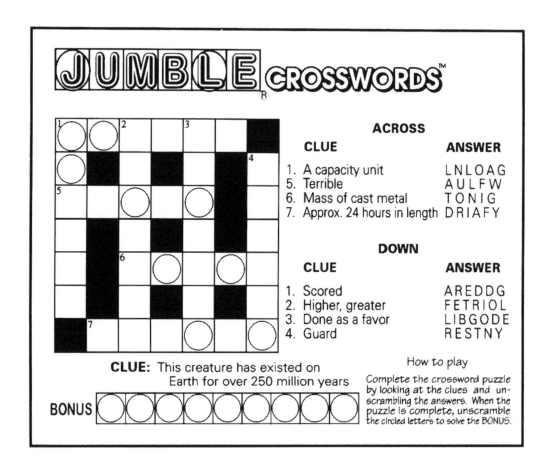

### ACROSS

| CLUE | ANSWER |
|------|--------|
| 1. A capacity unit | LNLOAG |
| 5. Terrible | AULFW |
| 6. Mass of cast metal | TONIG |
| 7. Approx. 24 hours in length | DRIAFY |

### DOWN

| CLUE | ANSWER |
|------|--------|
| 1. Scored | AREDDG |
| 2. Higher, greater | FETRIOL |
| 3. Done as a favor | LIBGODE |
| 4. Guard | RESTNY |

**CLUE:** This creature has existed on Earth for over 250 million years

BONUS ◯ ◯ ◯ ◯ ◯ ◯ ◯ ◯ ◯

### How to play

Complete the crossword puzzle by looking at the clues and unscrambling the answers. When the puzzle is complete, unscramble the circled letters to solve the BONUS.

#142

## JUMBLE CROSSWORDS™

### ACROSS

| CLUE | ANSWER |
|------|--------|
| 1. Pass | PALEES |
| 5. Pinch | RPICM |
| 6. Savory smell | RAAOM |
| 7. Tutor, coach | TENROM |

### DOWN

| CLUE | ANSWER |
|------|--------|
| 1. Extra | CXSSEE |
| 2. Disturb | TGTAEIA |
| 3. Defend as valid | STROPUP |
| 4. Damage | MAPIIR |

**CLUE:** Home to approx. 4 million

BONUS ○○○○○○○○○

How to play

Complete the crossword puzzle by looking at the clues and unscrambling the answers. When the puzzle is complete, unscramble the circled letters to solve the BONUS.

# #143

## JUMBLE CROSSWORDS™

### ACROSS

| CLUE | | ANSWER |
|------|---|--------|
| 1. | Plan | AADGNE |
| 5. | *Burnett* or *Rose* | RCLOA |
| 6. | Hang in the air | VREOH |
| 7. | Substantial | RUSTYD |

### DOWN

| CLUE | | ANSWER |
|------|---|--------|
| 1. | A TV "Bunker" | HIACRE |
| 2. | Range | AHRSETO |
| 3. | Hand over | LEDREIV |
| 4. | "_____ beloved..." | EADLRY |

**CLUE:** Conversation

**BONUS**

### How to play

Complete the crossword puzzle by looking at the clues and unscrambling the answers. When the puzzle is complete, unscramble the circled letters to solve the BONUS.

# PUZZLE #144

## JUMBLE CROSSWORDS™

### ACROSS

| CLUE | ANSWER |
|------|--------|
| 1. Weather map line | SIRAOB |
| 5. "_____ _____!" | REXAT |
| 6. Home to Augusta | EINAM |
| 7. Modifies | DANESM |

### DOWN

| CLUE | ANSWER |
|------|--------|
| 1. *The _____ Cometh* | MINECA |
| 2. Highest degree | TPMMIOU |
| 3. _____ *horse* | BRAANIA |
| 4. Rectangular boards | SLEAPN |

CLUE: *I have no chance of experiencing this*

BONUS
2 WORDS

How to play

Complete the crossword puzzle by looking at the clues and unscrambling the answers. When the puzzle is complete, unscramble the circled letters to solve the BONUS.

146

# JUMBLE CROSSWORDS™

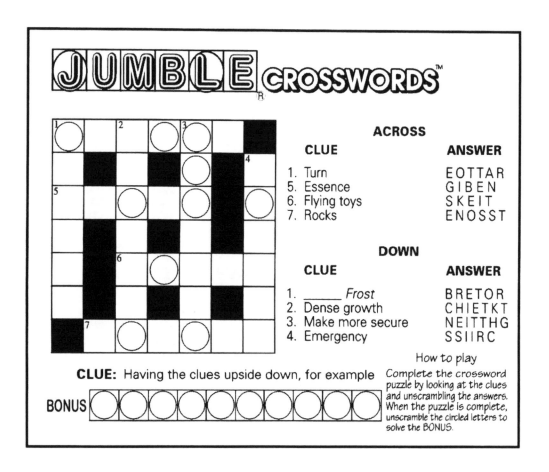

## ACROSS

| CLUE | ANSWER |
|------|--------|
| 1. Turn | EOTTAR |
| 5. Essence | GIBEN |
| 6. Flying toys | SKEIT |
| 7. Rocks | ENOSST |

## DOWN

| CLUE | ANSWER |
|------|--------|
| 1. _____ Frost | BRETOR |
| 2. Dense growth | CHIETKT |
| 3. Make more secure | NEITTHG |
| 4. Emergency | SSIIRC |

How to play

Complete the crossword puzzle by looking at the clues and unscrambling the answers. When the puzzle is complete, unscramble the circled letters to solve the BONUS.

**CLUE:** Having the clues upside down, for example

BONUS ◯◯◯◯◯◯◯◯◯◯

PUZZLE

#146

# JUMBLE CROSSWORDS™

## ACROSS

| CLUE | ANSWER |
|------|--------|
| 1. Turn | TRIDEV |
| 5. Leave | MASCR |
| 6. A city in Japan | OAASK |
| 7. Delicate | GTNEEL |

## DOWN

| CLUE | ANSWER |
|------|--------|
| 1. Disappointment | YDIAMS |
| 2. Wordy | BEROVES |
| 3. Widespread | PRAMTAN |
| 4. Expression of regard | GHMOAE |

CLUE: *I am one*

BONUS ◯◯◯◯◯◯◯◯

### How to play

Complete the crossword puzzle by looking at the clues and unscrambling the answers. When the puzzle is complete, unscramble the circled letters to solve the BONUS.

# #147

JUMBLE CROSSWORDS™

## ACROSS

| | CLUE | ANSWER |
|---|---|---|
| 1. | Approve | T P C E C A |
| 5. | Publish | S I E U S |
| 6. | Fool | O I D I T |
| 7. | Without question | N D I D E E |

## DOWN

| | CLUE | ANSWER |
|---|---|---|
| 1. | Each | E A I P E C |
| 2. | _____ Sea | S A A N I C P |
| 3. | Assumption | M E R P I E S |
| 4. | Scheduled | L S T A D E |

### How to play

Complete the crossword puzzle by looking at the clues and unscrambling the answers. When the puzzle is complete, unscramble the circled letters to solve the BONUS.

**CLUE:** Great

**BONUS** ○○○○○○○○

# #148

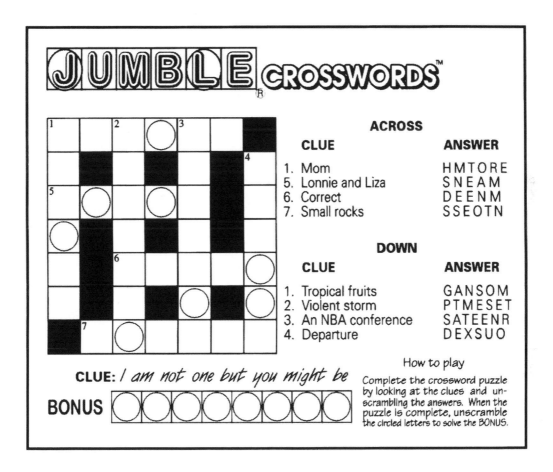

## JUMBLE CROSSWORDS™

### ACROSS

| | CLUE | ANSWER |
|---|---|---|
| 1. | Mom | HMTORE |
| 5. | Lonnie and Liza | SNEAM |
| 6. | Correct | DEENM |
| 7. | Small rocks | SSEOTN |

### DOWN

| | CLUE | ANSWER |
|---|---|---|
| 1. | Tropical fruits | GANSOM |
| 2. | Violent storm | PTMESET |
| 3. | An NBA conference | SATEENR |
| 4. | Departure | DEXSUO |

**CLUE:** *I am not one but you might be*

**BONUS** ○○○○○○○○

### How to play

Complete the crossword puzzle by looking at the clues and unscrambling the answers. When the puzzle is complete, unscramble the circled letters to solve the BONUS.

150

# #149

## JUMBLE CROSSWORDS™

### ACROSS

| CLUE | ANSWER |
|------|--------|
| 1. Shape | UPSTCL |
| 5. Leave | CMASR |
| 6. Record material | LVINY |
| 7. Edible kernel | DALNOM |

### DOWN

| CLUE | ANSWER |
|------|--------|
| 1. Small seed | EESSMA |
| 2. Fall apart | RUNLEAV |
| 3. _____ cheese | MOTNEIP |
| 4. Movable fold of skin | LEEDIY |

CLUE: *I've never had one*

BONUS

### How to play

Complete the crossword puzzle by looking at the clues and unscrambling the answers. When the puzzle is complete, unscramble the circled letters to solve the BONUS.

# PUZZLE

# #150

## JUMBLE CROSSWORDS™

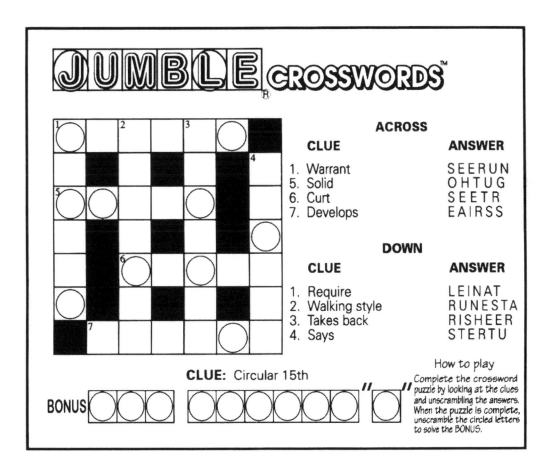

### ACROSS

| CLUE | ANSWER |
| --- | --- |
| 1. Warrant | SEERUN |
| 5. Solid | OHTUG |
| 6. Curt | SEETR |
| 7. Develops | EAIRSS |

### DOWN

| CLUE | ANSWER |
| --- | --- |
| 1. Require | LEINAT |
| 2. Walking style | RUNESTA |
| 3. Takes back | RISHEER |
| 4. Says | STERTU |

**CLUE:** Circular 15th

**BONUS** ◯◯◯ ◯◯◯◯◯◯ "◯"

### How to play

Complete the crossword puzzle by looking at the clues and unscrambling the answers. When the puzzle is complete, unscramble the circled letters to solve the BONUS.

152

# PUZZLE

# #151

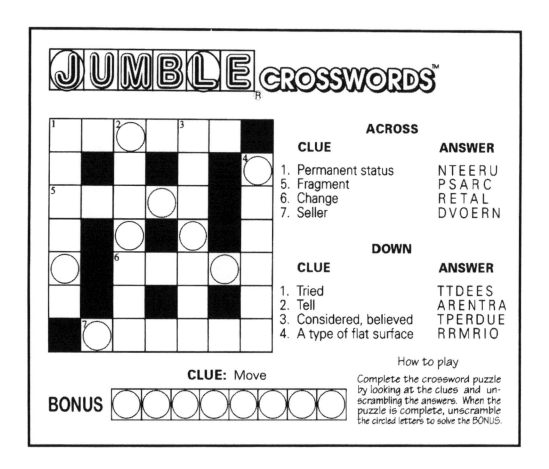

# JUMBLE CROSSWORDS™

## ACROSS

| CLUE | ANSWER |
|------|--------|
| 1. Permanent status | N T E E R U |
| 5. Fragment | P S A R C |
| 6. Change | R E T A L |
| 7. Seller | D V O E R N |

## DOWN

| CLUE | ANSWER |
|------|--------|
| 1. Tried | T T D E E S |
| 2. Tell | A R E N T R A |
| 3. Considered, believed | T P E R D U E |
| 4. A type of flat surface | R R M R I O |

### How to play

Complete the crossword puzzle by looking at the clues and unscrambling the answers. When the puzzle is complete, unscramble the circled letters to solve the BONUS.

**CLUE:** Move

**BONUS**

153

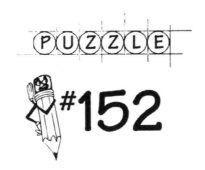

# PUZZLE

## #152

# JUMBLE CROSSWORDS™

## ACROSS

| CLUE | ANSWER |
|------|--------|
| 1. A type of baby | GLPEIT |
| 5. Decipher | VSELO |
| 6. Ridge | GDLEE |
| 7. Amazement | DWNORE |

## DOWN

| CLUE | ANSWER |
|------|--------|
| 1. Engine part | STPNIO |
| 2. He lived from 1564 - 1642 | ALIEOLG |
| 3. Changed | EDMNEED |
| 4. Seem | EAAPPR |

### How to play

Complete the crossword puzzle by looking at the clues and unscrambling the answers. When the puzzle is complete, unscramble the circled letters to solve the BONUS.

CLUE: *I was born in* _____ _____

BONUS
2 WORDS

# PUZZLE #153

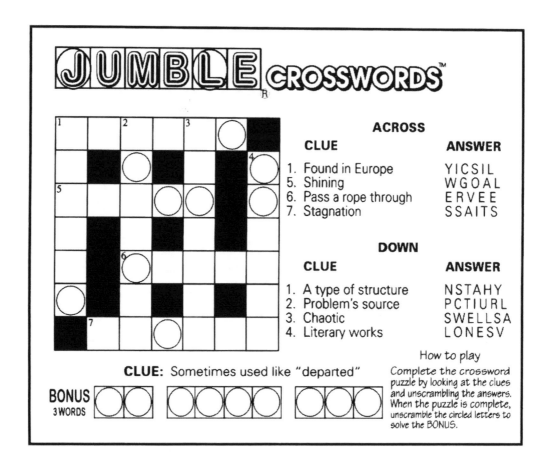

## JUMBLE CROSSWORDS™

### ACROSS

| CLUE | ANSWER |
|------|--------|
| 1. Found in Europe | YICSIL |
| 5. Shining | WGOAL |
| 6. Pass a rope through | ERVEE |
| 7. Stagnation | SSAITS |

### DOWN

| CLUE | ANSWER |
|------|--------|
| 1. A type of structure | NSTAHY |
| 2. Problem's source | PCTIURL |
| 3. Chaotic | SWELLSA |
| 4. Literary works | LONESV |

**How to play**

Complete the crossword puzzle by looking at the clues and unscrambling the answers. When the puzzle is complete, unscramble the circled letters to solve the BONUS.

**CLUE:** Sometimes used like "departed"

**BONUS**
3 WORDS

155

# #154

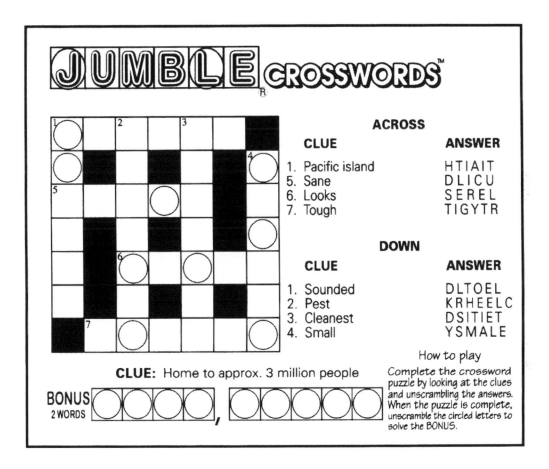

## JUMBLE CROSSWORDS™

### ACROSS

| CLUE | ANSWER |
|------|--------|
| 1. Pacific island | HTIAIT |
| 5. Sane | DLICU |
| 6. Looks | SEREL |
| 7. Tough | TIGYTR |

### DOWN

| CLUE | ANSWER |
|------|--------|
| 1. Sounded | DLTOEL |
| 2. Pest | KRHEELC |
| 3. Cleanest | DSITIET |
| 4. Small | YSMALE |

**How to play**

Complete the crossword puzzle by looking at the clues and unscrambling the answers. When the puzzle is complete, unscramble the circled letters to solve the BONUS.

**CLUE:** Home to approx. 3 million people

BONUS
2 WORDS

○○○○ , ○○○○○

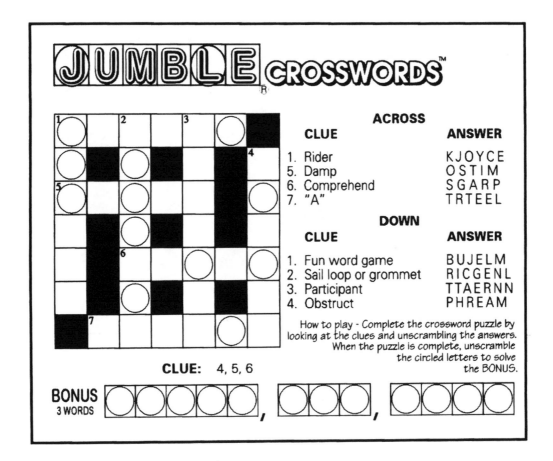

## JUMBLE CROSSWORDS™

### ACROSS

| CLUE | ANSWER |
|------|--------|
| 1. Rider | KJOYCE |
| 5. Damp | OSTIM |
| 6. Comprehend | SGARP |
| 7. "A" | TRTEEL |

### DOWN

| CLUE | ANSWER |
|------|--------|
| 1. Fun word game | BUJELM |
| 2. Sail loop or grommet | RICGENL |
| 3. Participant | TTAERNN |
| 4. Obstruct | PHREAM |

How to play - Complete the crossword puzzle by looking at the clues and unscrambling the answers. When the puzzle is complete, unscramble the circled letters to solve the BONUS.

CLUE: 4, 5, 6

BONUS
3 WORDS

◯◯◯◯◯ , ◯◯◯ , ◯◯◯◯

# #156

## JUMBLE CROSSWORDS™

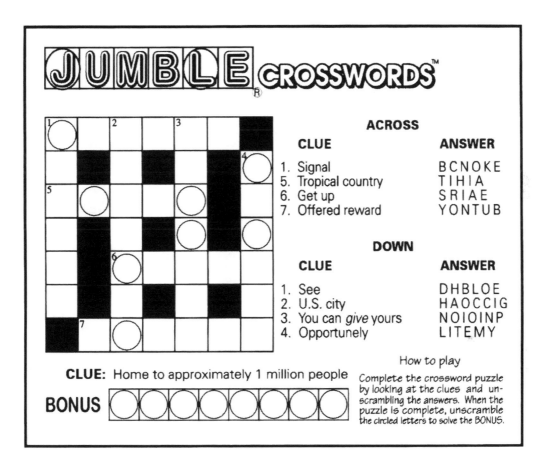

### ACROSS

| CLUE | ANSWER |
|------|--------|
| 1. Signal | BCNOKE |
| 5. Tropical country | TIHIA |
| 6. Get up | SRIAE |
| 7. Offered reward | YONTUB |

### DOWN

| CLUE | ANSWER |
|------|--------|
| 1. See | DHBLOE |
| 2. U.S. city | HAOCCIG |
| 3. You can *give* yours | NOIOINP |
| 4. Opportunely | LITEMY |

**How to play**

Complete the crossword puzzle by looking at the clues and unscrambling the answers. When the puzzle is complete, unscramble the circled letters to solve the BONUS.

**CLUE:** Home to approximately 1 million people

**BONUS** ◯◯◯◯◯◯◯◯

# #157

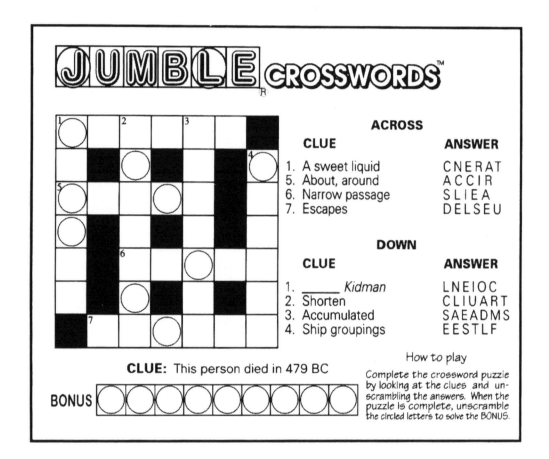

## JUMBLE CROSSWORDS™

### ACROSS

| CLUE | ANSWER |
|---|---|
| 1. A sweet liquid | C N E R A T |
| 5. About, around | A C C I R |
| 6. Narrow passage | S L I E A |
| 7. Escapes | D E L S E U |

### DOWN

| CLUE | ANSWER |
|---|---|
| 1. _____ Kidman | L N E I O C |
| 2. Shorten | C L I U A R T |
| 3. Accumulated | S A E A D M S |
| 4. Ship groupings | E E S T L F |

**CLUE:** This person died in 479 BC

BONUS

### How to play

Complete the crossword puzzle by looking at the clues and unscrambling the answers. When the puzzle is complete, unscramble the circled letters to solve the BONUS.

# PUZZLE #158

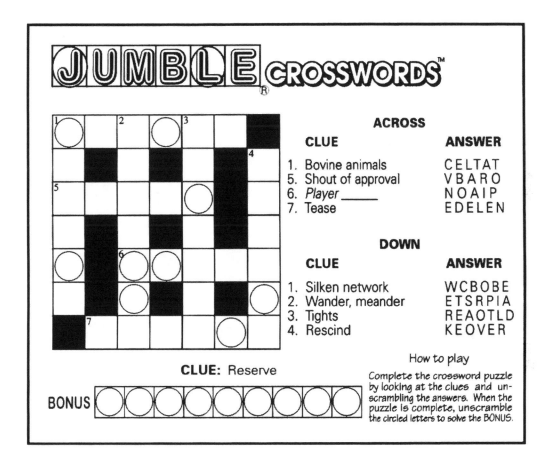

## JUMBLE CROSSWORDS™

### ACROSS

| CLUE | ANSWER |
|------|--------|
| 1. Bovine animals | CELTAT |
| 5. Shout of approval | VBARO |
| 6. *Player* _____ | NOAIP |
| 7. Tease | EDELEN |

### DOWN

| CLUE | ANSWER |
|------|--------|
| 1. Silken network | WCBOBE |
| 2. Wander, meander | ETSRPIA |
| 3. Tights | REAOTLD |
| 4. Rescind | KEOVER |

**How to play**

Complete the crossword puzzle by looking at the clues and unscrambling the answers. When the puzzle is complete, unscramble the circled letters to solve the BONUS.

**CLUE:** Reserve

BONUS

# #159

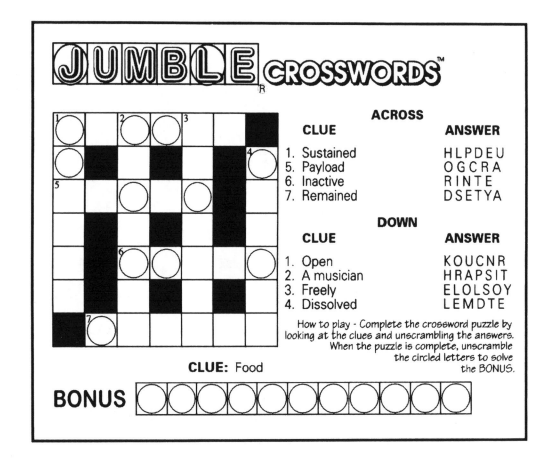

## JUMBLE CROSSWORDS™

### ACROSS

| CLUE | ANSWER |
|------|--------|
| 1. Sustained | HLPDEU |
| 5. Payload | OGCRA |
| 6. Inactive | RINTE |
| 7. Remained | DSETYA |

### DOWN

| CLUE | ANSWER |
|------|--------|
| 1. Open | KOUCNR |
| 2. A musician | HRAPSIT |
| 3. Freely | ELOLSOY |
| 4. Dissolved | LEMDTE |

How to play - Complete the crossword puzzle by looking at the clues and unscrambling the answers. When the puzzle is complete, unscramble the circled letters to solve the BONUS.

**CLUE:** Food

**BONUS**

# #160

## JUMBLE CROSSWORDS™

### ACROSS

| CLUE | ANSWER |
|---|---|
| 1. Circular ornament | TWAREH |
| 5. Measuring device | RRLEU |
| 6. Hit | NUPDO |
| 7. Only a male can be one | PWNEEH |

### DOWN

| CLUE | ANSWER |
|---|---|
| 1. Heat | MWRAHT |
| 2. Total _____ | PISEECL |
| 3. By way of | GTORHHU |
| 4. Follow | OSWHAD |

**How to play**

Complete the crossword puzzle by looking at the clues and unscrambling the answers. When the puzzle is complete, unscramble the circled letters to solve the BONUS.

**CLUE:** *"I am one...You may or may not be"*

**BONUS** ◯◯◯◯◯ - ◯◯

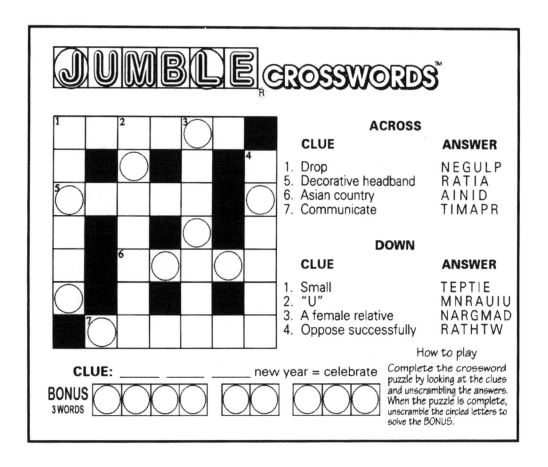

# PUZZLE

# #161

## JUMBLE CROSSWORDS™

### ACROSS

| CLUE | ANSWER |
|------|--------|
| 1. Drop | NEGULP |
| 5. Decorative headband | RATIA |
| 6. Asian country | AINID |
| 7. Communicate | TIMAPR |

### DOWN

| CLUE | ANSWER |
|------|--------|
| 1. Small | TEPTIE |
| 2. "U" | MNRAUIU |
| 3. A female relative | NARGMAD |
| 4. Oppose successfully | RATHTW |

### How to play

Complete the crossword puzzle by looking at the clues and unscrambling the answers. When the puzzle is complete, unscramble the circled letters to solve the BONUS.

CLUE: _____ _____ _____ new year = celebrate

BONUS
3 WORDS

# PUZZLE #162

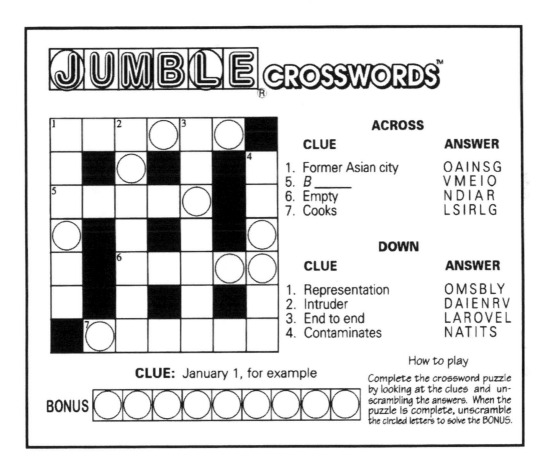

## JUMBLE CROSSWORDS™

### ACROSS

| CLUE | ANSWER |
|------|--------|
| 1. Former Asian city | O A I N S G |
| 5. *B* _____ | V M E I O |
| 6. Empty | N D I A R |
| 7. Cooks | L S I R L G |

### DOWN

| CLUE | ANSWER |
|------|--------|
| 1. Representation | O M S B L Y |
| 2. Intruder | D A I E N R V |
| 3. End to end | L A R O V E L |
| 4. Contaminates | N A T I T S |

### How to play

Complete the crossword puzzle by looking at the clues and unscrambling the answers. When the puzzle is complete, unscramble the circled letters to solve the BONUS.

**CLUE:** January 1, for example

BONUS

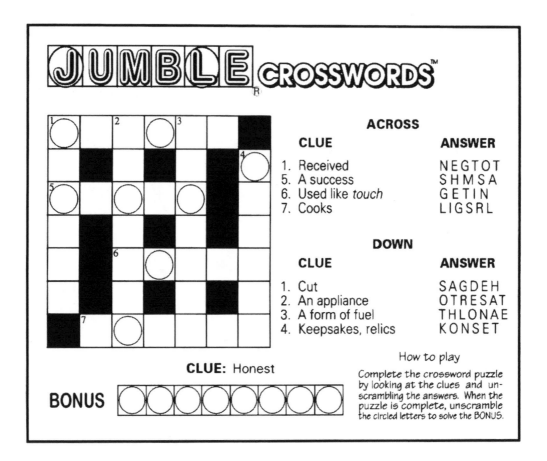

JUMBLE CROSSWORDS™

**ACROSS**

| CLUE | ANSWER |
|------|--------|
| 1. Received | N E G T O T |
| 5. A success | S H M S A |
| 6. Used like *touch* | G E T I N |
| 7. Cooks | L I G S R L |

**DOWN**

| CLUE | ANSWER |
|------|--------|
| 1. Cut | S A G D E H |
| 2. An appliance | O T R E S A T |
| 3. A form of fuel | T H L O N A E |
| 4. Keepsakes, relics | K O N S E T |

How to play

Complete the crossword puzzle by looking at the clues and un-scrambling the answers. When the puzzle is complete, unscramble the circled letters to solve the BONUS.

**CLUE:** Honest

BONUS

165

# JUMBLE CROSSWORDS™

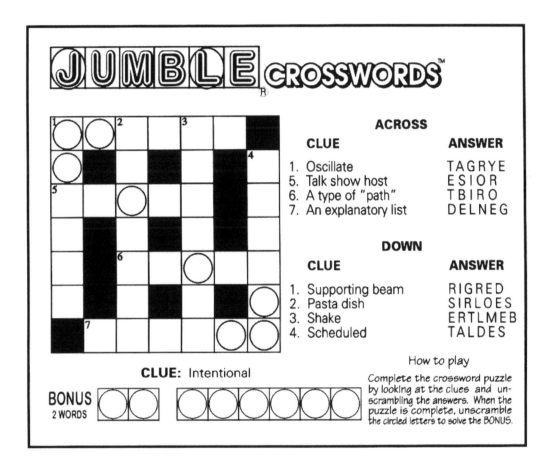

## ACROSS

| CLUE | ANSWER |
|------|--------|
| 1. Oscillate | TAGRYE |
| 5. Talk show host | ESIOR |
| 6. A type of "path" | TBIRO |
| 7. An explanatory list | DELNEG |

## DOWN

| CLUE | ANSWER |
|------|--------|
| 1. Supporting beam | RIGRED |
| 2. Pasta dish | SIRLOES |
| 3. Shake | ERTLMEB |
| 4. Scheduled | TALDES |

**How to play**

Complete the crossword puzzle by looking at the clues and unscrambling the answers. When the puzzle is complete, unscramble the circled letters to solve the BONUS.

**CLUE:** Intentional

**BONUS**
2 WORDS

# MORE JUMBLE CROSSWORDS

## DOUBLE BONUS PUZZLES

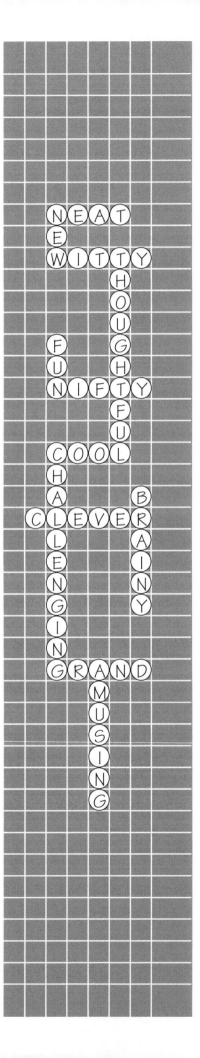

# #165

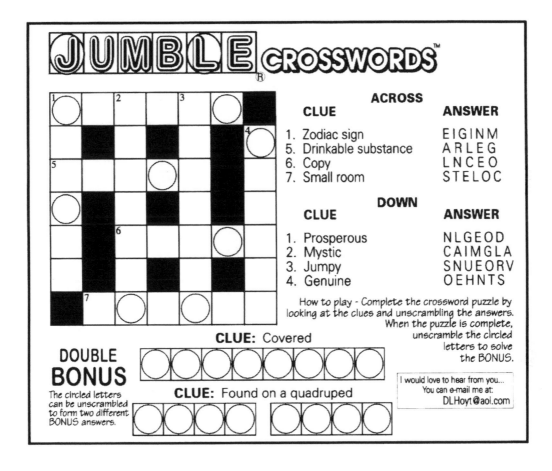

## JUMBLE CROSSWORDS™

### ACROSS

| CLUE | | ANSWER |
|---|---|---|
| 1. | Zodiac sign | E I G I N M |
| 5. | Drinkable substance | A R L E G |
| 6. | Copy | L N C E O |
| 7. | Small room | S T E L O C |

### DOWN

| CLUE | | ANSWER |
|---|---|---|
| 1. | Prosperous | N L G E O D |
| 2. | Mystic | C A I M G L A |
| 3. | Jumpy | S N U E O R V |
| 4. | Genuine | O E H N T S |

How to play - Complete the crossword puzzle by looking at the clues and unscrambling the answers. When the puzzle is complete, unscramble the circled letters to solve the BONUS.

**CLUE:** Covered

**DOUBLE BONUS**

The circled letters can be unscrambled to form two different BONUS answers.

**CLUE:** Found on a quadruped

I would love to hear from you... You can e-mail me at: DLHoyt@aol.com

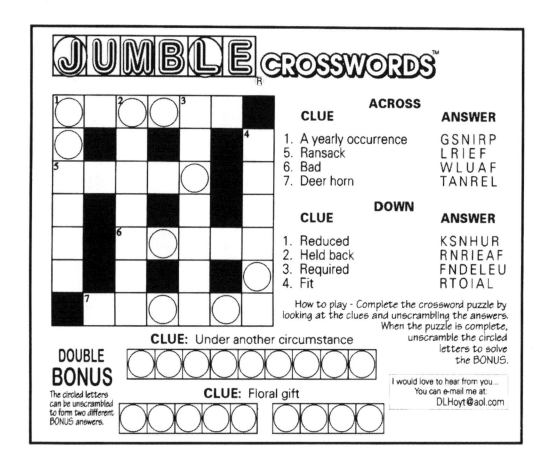

# JUMBLE CROSSWORDS™

## ACROSS

| CLUE | ANSWER |
|------|--------|
| 1. A yearly occurrence | G S N I R P |
| 5. Ransack | L R I E F |
| 6. Bad | W L U A F |
| 7. Deer horn | T A N R E L |

## DOWN

| CLUE | ANSWER |
|------|--------|
| 1. Reduced | K S N H U R |
| 2. Held back | R N R I E A F |
| 3. Required | F N D E L E U |
| 4. Fit | R T O I A L |

How to play - Complete the crossword puzzle by looking at the clues and unscrambling the answers. When the puzzle is complete, unscramble the circled letters to solve the BONUS.

I would love to hear from you...
You can e-mail me at:
DLHoyt@aol.com

**CLUE:** Under another circumstance

**DOUBLE BONUS**

The circled letters can be unscrambled to form two different BONUS answers.

**CLUE:** Floral gift

169

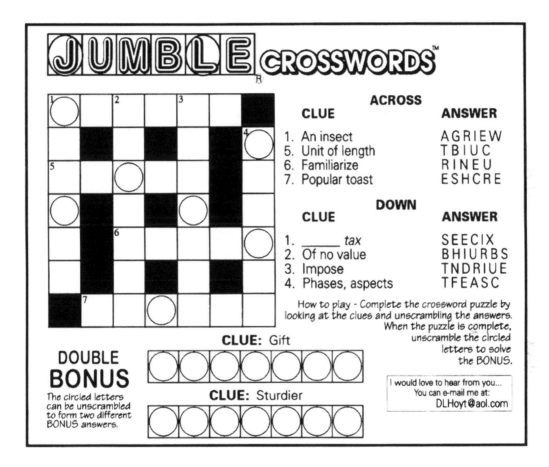

# JUMBLE CROSSWORDS™

**ACROSS**

| CLUE | ANSWER |
|------|--------|
| 1. An insect | A G R I E W |
| 5. Unit of length | T B I U C |
| 6. Familiarize | R I N E U |
| 7. Popular toast | E S H C R E |

**DOWN**

| CLUE | ANSWER |
|------|--------|
| 1. _____ tax | S E E C I X |
| 2. Of no value | B H I U R B S |
| 3. Impose | T N D R I U E |
| 4. Phases, aspects | T F E A S C |

How to play - Complete the crossword puzzle by looking at the clues and unscrambling the answers. When the puzzle is complete, unscramble the circled letters to solve the BONUS.

I would love to hear from you... You can e-mail me at: DLHoyt@aol.com

**CLUE:** Gift

**DOUBLE BONUS**

The circled letters can be unscrambled to form two different BONUS answers.

**CLUE:** Sturdier

## PUZZLE #168

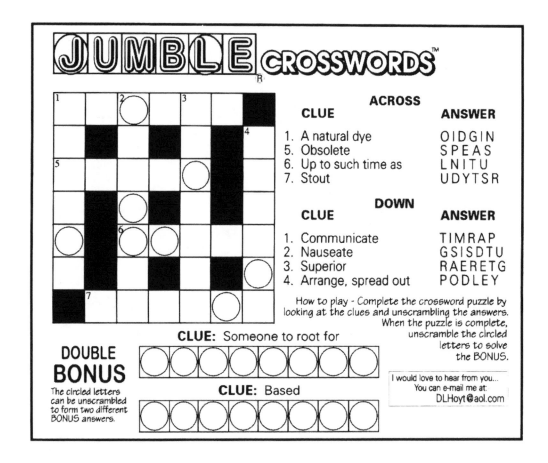

# JUMBLE CROSSWORDS™

### ACROSS

| CLUE | | ANSWER |
|---|---|---|
| 1. | A natural dye | OIDGIN |
| 5. | Obsolete | SPEAS |
| 6. | Up to such time as | LNITU |
| 7. | Stout | UDYTSR |

### DOWN

| CLUE | | ANSWER |
|---|---|---|
| 1. | Communicate | TIMRAP |
| 2. | Nauseate | GSISDTU |
| 3. | Superior | RAERETG |
| 4. | Arrange, spread out | PODLEY |

How to play - Complete the crossword puzzle by looking at the clues and unscrambling the answers. When the puzzle is complete, unscramble the circled letters to solve the BONUS.

**DOUBLE BONUS**

The circled letters can be unscrambled to form two different BONUS answers.

**CLUE:** Someone to root for

**CLUE:** Based

I would love to hear from you... You can e-mail me at: DLHoyt@aol.com

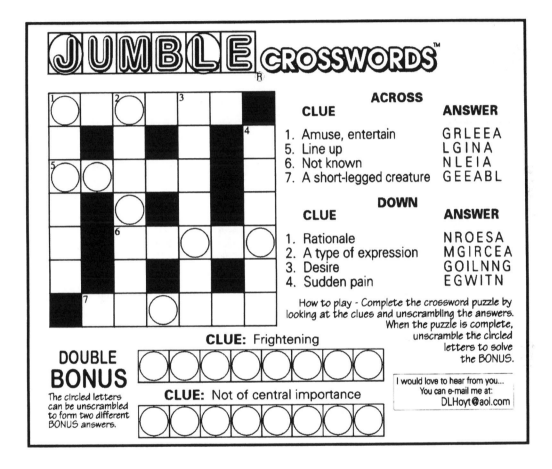

# JUMBLE CROSSWORDS™

## ACROSS

| CLUE | ANSWER |
|------|--------|
| 1. Amuse, entertain | GRLEEA |
| 5. Line up | LGINA |
| 6. Not known | NLEIA |
| 7. A short-legged creature | GEEABL |

## DOWN

| CLUE | ANSWER |
|------|--------|
| 1. Rationale | NROESA |
| 2. A type of expression | MGIRCEA |
| 3. Desire | GOILNNG |
| 4. Sudden pain | EGWITN |

How to play - Complete the crossword puzzle by looking at the clues and unscrambling the answers. When the puzzle is complete, unscramble the circled letters to solve the BONUS.

**CLUE:** Frightening

**DOUBLE BONUS**

The circled letters can be unscrambled to form two different BONUS answers.

**CLUE:** Not of central importance

I would love to hear from you...
You can e-mail me at:
DLHoyt@aol.com

172

# PUZZLE

# #170

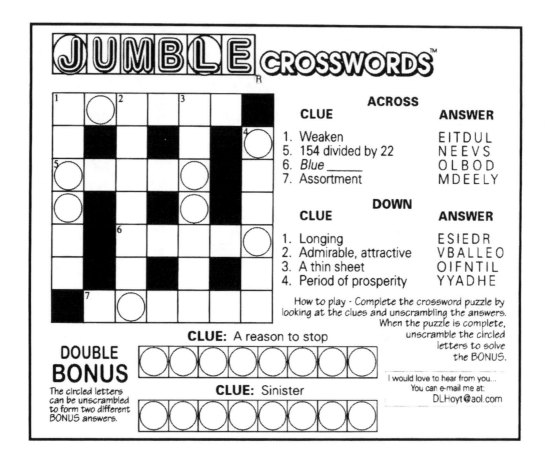

## JUMBLE CROSSWORDS™

### ACROSS

| CLUE | ANSWER |
|---|---|
| 1. Weaken | E I T D U L |
| 5. 154 divided by 22 | N E E V S |
| 6. *Blue* _____ | O L B O D |
| 7. Assortment | M D E E L Y |

### DOWN

| CLUE | ANSWER |
|---|---|
| 1. Longing | E S I E D R |
| 2. Admirable, attractive | V B A L L E O |
| 3. A thin sheet | O I F N T I L |
| 4. Period of prosperity | Y Y A D H E |

*How to play - Complete the crossword puzzle by looking at the clues and unscrambling the answers. When the puzzle is complete, unscramble the circled letters to solve the BONUS.*

**CLUE:** A reason to stop

## DOUBLE BONUS

The circled letters can be unscrambled to form two different BONUS answers.

**CLUE:** Sinister

I would love to hear from you...
You can e-mail me at:
DLHoyt@aol.com

# #171

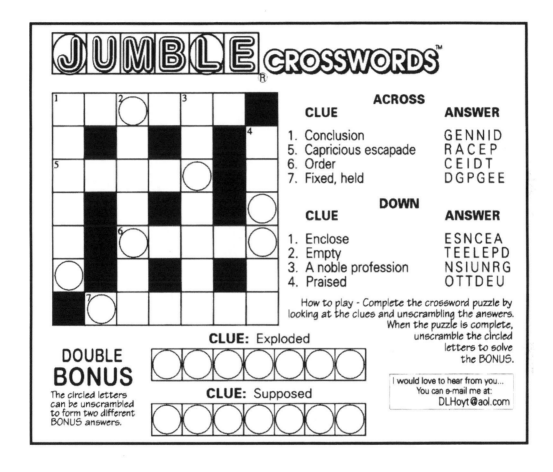

## JUMBLE CROSSWORDS™

### ACROSS

| CLUE | ANSWER |
|------|--------|
| 1. Conclusion | GENNID |
| 5. Capricious escapade | RACEP |
| 6. Order | CEIDT |
| 7. Fixed, held | DGPGEE |

### DOWN

| CLUE | ANSWER |
|------|--------|
| 1. Enclose | ESNCEA |
| 2. Empty | TEELEPD |
| 3. A noble profession | NSIUNRG |
| 4. Praised | OTTDEU |

How to play - Complete the crossword puzzle by looking at the clues and unscrambling the answers. When the puzzle is complete, unscramble the circled letters to solve the BONUS.

**DOUBLE BONUS**
The circled letters can be unscrambled to form two different BONUS answers.

**CLUE:** Exploded

**CLUE:** Supposed

I would love to hear from you...
You can e-mail me at:
DLHoyt@aol.com

# PUZZLE

# #172

## JUMBLE CROSSWORDS™

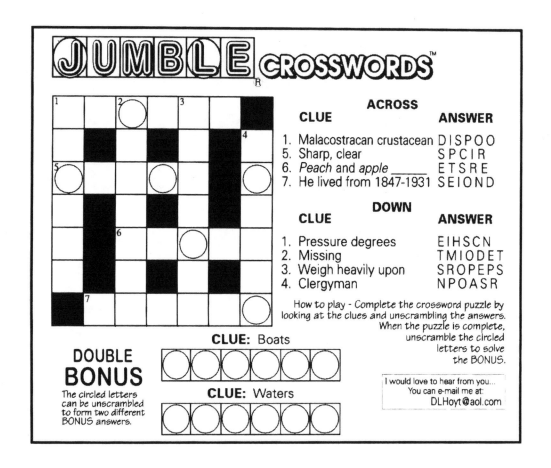

### ACROSS

| CLUE | | ANSWER |
|------|---|--------|
| 1. | Malacostracan crustacean | DISPOO |
| 5. | Sharp, clear | SPCIR |
| 6. | *Peach* and *apple* _____ | ETSRE |
| 7. | He lived from 1847-1931 | SEIOND |

### DOWN

| CLUE | | ANSWER |
|------|---|--------|
| 1. | Pressure degrees | EIHSCN |
| 2. | Missing | TMIODET |
| 3. | Weigh heavily upon | SROPEPS |
| 4. | Clergyman | NPOASR |

How to play - Complete the crossword puzzle by looking at the clues and unscrambling the answers. When the puzzle is complete, unscramble the circled letters to solve the BONUS.

**CLUE:** Boats

**DOUBLE BONUS**

The circled letters can be unscrambled to form two different BONUS answers.

**CLUE:** Waters

I would love to hear from you...
You can e-mail me at:
DLHoyt@aol.com

175

 #173

# JUMBLE CROSSWORDS™

### ACROSS

| CLUE | ANSWER |
|---|---|
| 1. Packing instrument | RRDOAM |
| 5. Therefore | CHEEN |
| 6. Apportion | TLLOA |
| 7. Try | EPASLM |

### DOWN

| CLUE | ANSWER |
|---|---|
| 1. Discuss again | HHAERS |
| 2. Home to approx. 800,000 | TNAAONM |
| 3. Cover a portion | PAVROLE |
| 4. Walking style | EPIOTT |

## DOUBLE BONUS

**CLUE:** Stupid

○○○○○○○

The circled letters can be unscrambled to form two different BONUS answers.

**CLUE:** A Greek letter

○○○○○○○

How to play
Complete the crossword puzzle by looking at the clues and unscrambling the answers.
When the puzzle is complete, unscramble the circled letters to solve the Bonus.

# #174

## JUMBLE CROSSWORDS™

### ACROSS

| CLUE | ANSWER |
|------|--------|
| 1. An island capital | U S N A A S |
| 5. Guiding principle | D E R O C |
| 6. By surprise | C A A K B |
| 7. Fame | W R N N E O |

### DOWN

| CLUE | ANSWER |
|------|--------|
| 1. Chipped | C I N D E K |
| 2. Ooze | P E G A E S E |
| 3. A tropical fruit | D O O A C A V |
| 4. Disgust | C I E K N S |

**DOUBLE BONUS**

The circled letters can be unscrambled to form two different BONUS answers.

**CLUE:** Position

**CLUE:** Intrudes

How to play
Complete the crossword puzzle by looking at the clues and unscrambling the answers.
When the puzzle is complete, unscramble the circled letters to solve the Bonus.

# #175

## JUMBLE CROSSWORDS™

| | ACROSS | |
|---|---|---|
| **CLUE** | | **ANSWER** |
| 1. Hang | | DELAGN |
| 5. Deserve | | MTIER |
| 6. Lead | | HREUS |
| 7. Rectified | | DDEENM |

| | DOWN | |
|---|---|---|
| **CLUE** | | **ANSWER** |
| 1. Break | | DEGAAM |
| 2. Cultivate | | RNUTEUR |
| 3. Fastened | | TLCADHE |
| 4. Hot | | OIDRRT |

**DOUBLE BONUS**

The circled letters can be unscrambled to form two different BONUS answers.

**CLUE:** Reduced
◯◯◯◯◯◯◯

**CLUE:** A halfway point
◯◯◯ - ◯◯◯◯

How to play
Complete the crossword puzzle by looking at the clues and unscrambling the answers. When the puzzle is complete, unscramble the circled letters to solve the Bonus.

# JUMBLE CROSSWORDS™

## ACROSS

| CLUE | ANSWER |
|------|--------|
| 1. Red or white _____ | RSUPEC |
| 5. A woman's name | HCTAY |
| 6. Inn | LETHO |
| 7. Building material | CSUOCT |

## DOWN

| CLUE | ANSWER |
|------|--------|
| 1. Cordial | CSIAOL |
| 2. A type of mechanism | THARTEC |
| 3. Mystifying | CCTIYRP |
| 4. Greek and Roman god | LLAOOP |

## DOUBLE BONUS

The circled letters can be unscrambled to form two different BONUS answers.

**CLUE:** Roughest

**CLUE:** Whips

How to play
Complete the crossword puzzle by looking at the clues and unscrambling the answers.
When the puzzle is complete, unscramble the circled letters to solve the Bonus.

# #177

# JUMBLE CROSSWORDS™

### ACROSS

| CLUE | ANSWER |
|------|--------|
| 1. A rodent | RPHEOG |
| 5. Recess | EIHNC |
| 6. Catastrophic | FLAAT |
| 7. Lambaste | CSHROC |

### DOWN

| CLUE | ANSWER |
|------|--------|
| 1. Aristocracy | TERYGN |
| 2. Largest of its kind | CAIPFIC |
| 3. Builder | REROTCE |
| 4. Resources | EHWTLA |

## DOUBLE BONUS

The circled letters can be unscrambled to form two different BONUS answers.

**CLUE:** Building material

◯◯◯◯◯◯◯

**CLUE:** Deliberate spin

◯◯◯◯◯◯◯

How to play
Complete the crossword puzzle by looking at the clues and unscrambling the answers.
When the puzzle is complete, unscramble the circled letters to solve the Bonus.

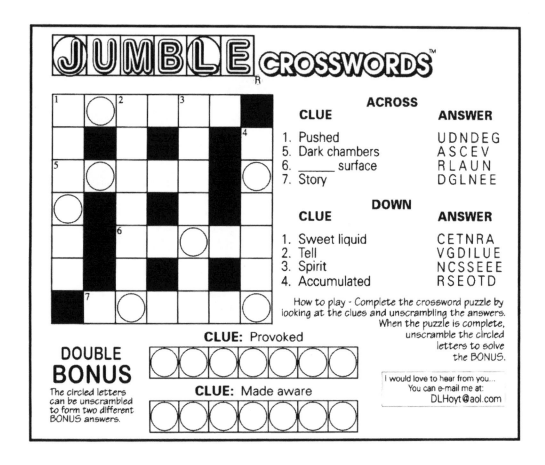

## JUMBLE CROSSWORDS™

### ACROSS

| CLUE | ANSWER |
|------|--------|
| 1. Pushed | U D N D E G |
| 5. Dark chambers | A S C E V |
| 6. _____ surface | R L A U N |
| 7. Story | D G L N E E |

### DOWN

| CLUE | ANSWER |
|------|--------|
| 1. Sweet liquid | C E T N R A |
| 2. Tell | V G D I L U E |
| 3. Spirit | N C S S E E E |
| 4. Accumulated | R S E O T D |

How to play - Complete the crossword puzzle by looking at the clues and unscrambling the answers. When the puzzle is complete, unscramble the circled letters to solve the BONUS.

**CLUE:** Provoked

**DOUBLE BONUS**

The circled letters can be unscrambled to form two different BONUS answers.

**CLUE:** Made aware

I would love to hear from you... You can e-mail me at: DLHoyt@aol.com

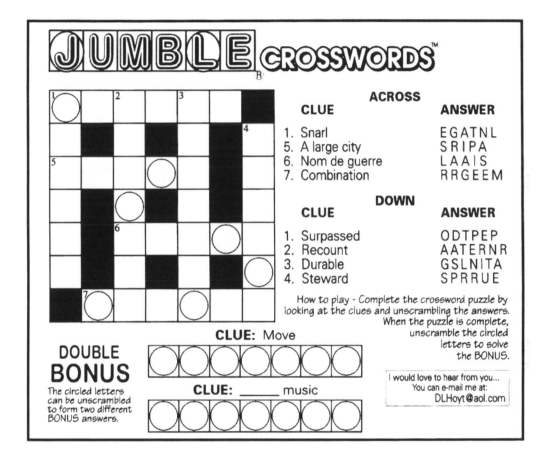

# JUMBLE CROSSWORDS™

## ACROSS

| CLUE | ANSWER |
|------|--------|
| 1. Snarl | EGATNL |
| 5. A large city | SRIPA |
| 6. Nom de guerre | LAAIS |
| 7. Combination | RRGEEM |

## DOWN

| CLUE | ANSWER |
|------|--------|
| 1. Surpassed | ODTPEP |
| 2. Recount | AATERNR |
| 3. Durable | GSLNITA |
| 4. Steward | SPRRUE |

How to play - Complete the crossword puzzle by looking at the clues and unscrambling the answers. When the puzzle is complete, unscramble the circled letters to solve the BONUS.

**DOUBLE BONUS**

The circled letters can be unscrambled to form two different BONUS answers.

**CLUE:** Move

**CLUE:** _____ music

I would love to hear from you... You can e-mail me at: DLHoyt@aol.com

# #180

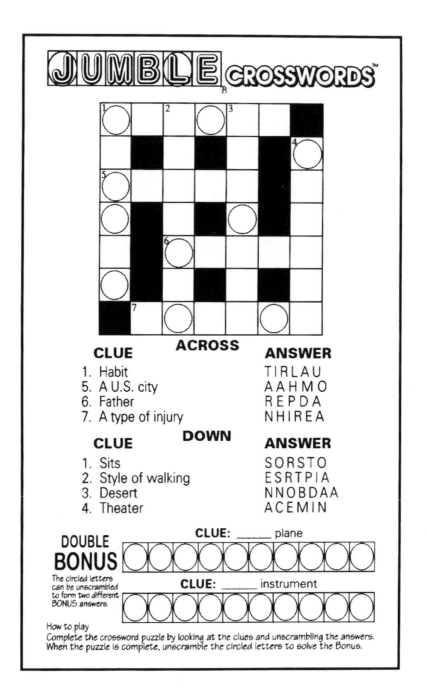

## JUMBLE CROSSWORDS™

### ACROSS

| CLUE | ANSWER |
|------|--------|
| 1. Habit | TIRLAU |
| 5. A U.S. city | AAHMO |
| 6. Father | REPDA |
| 7. A type of injury | NHIREA |

### DOWN

| CLUE | ANSWER |
|------|--------|
| 1. Sits | SORSTO |
| 2. Style of walking | ESRTPIA |
| 3. Desert | NNOBDAA |
| 4. Theater | ACEMIN |

**DOUBLE BONUS**

The circled letters can be unscrambled to form two different BONUS answers.

CLUE: _____ plane

CLUE: _____ instrument

How to play
Complete the crossword puzzle by looking at the clues and unscrambling the answers.
When the puzzle is complete, unscramble the circled letters to solve the Bonus.

183

# ANSWERS

1. **Answers:**
   1A—THREAT 5A—ALTAR 6A—LUBED 7A—WRITER
   1D—THAWED 2D—RATTLER 3D—ACROBAT 4D—KINDER
   **Bonus:** Difficult to deal with—AWKWARD

2. **Answers:**
   1A—AFRICA 5A—NIGEL 6A—INNER 7A—WESLEY
   1D—ARNOLD 2D—RAGTIME 3D—COLONEL 4D—NEARBY
   **Bonus:** Wayne Knight played this character—NEWMAN

3. **Answers:**
   1A—ANTHEM 5A—SPENT 6A—AMUSE 7A—OLDEST
   1D—ASSIST 2D—TOENAIL 3D—ENTHUSE 4D—LOWEST
   **Bonus:** You are working on one now—SOLUTION

4. **Answers:**
   1A—PACIFY 5A—NOTES 6A—INJURE 7A—CHEESY
   1D—PUNISH 2D—CATFISH 3D—FISSURE 4D—LIKELY
   **Bonus:** Long associated with the name "George"—YANKEES

5. **Answers:**
   1A—ORANGE 5A—ADAGE 6A—ARSON 7A—STODGY
   1D—ORACLE 2D—ADAMANT 3D—GUESSED 4D—WHINNY
   **Bonus:** Not specified—SOMEHOW

6. **Answers:**
   1A—MOBILE 5A—LUCID 6A—CLIMB 7A—BEAGLE
   1D—MELLOW 2D—BICYCLE 3D—LODGING 4D—NIMBLE
   **Bonus:** There was one in *Beetlejuice*, and another in *Sliver*—BALDWIN

7. **Answers:**
   1A—BUDDHA 5A—CRYUS 6A—BLACK 7A—FEWEST
   1D—BECOME 2D—DURABLE 3D—HOSTAGE 4D—BUCKET
   **Bonus:** Yours is welcomed—FEEDBACK

8. **Answers:**
   1A—MISFIT 5A—SHOES 6A—MEDAL 7A—INGRID
   1D—MUSTER 2D—SHOWMAN 3D—INSIDER 4D—VEILED
   **Bonus:** Classic—VINTAGE

9. **Answers:**
   1A—INLAND 5A—MINUS 6A—EARTH 7A—ITALIC
   1D—INMATE 2D—LENIENT 3D—NOSTRIL 4D—GOTHIC
   **Bonus:** A reason to take a seat—HAIRCUT

10. **Answers:**
    1A—ASSUME 5A—PLANE 6A—RATIO 7A—SWOOPS
    1D—ALPINE 2D—SPARROW 3D—MAESTRO 4D—VENOUS
    **Bonus:** Born in 1769, died in 1821—NAPOLEON

11. **Answers:**
    1A—KELLEY 5A—SLUNG 6A—GRIND 7A—GRAHAM
    1D—KISSES 2D—LOUNGER 3D—ENGLISH 4D—WISDOM
    **Bonus:** Gives abundantly—SHOWERS

12. **Answers:**
    1A—PILLOW 5A—MANET 6A—EMEND 7A—STOLEN
    1D—PAMELA 2D—LONGEST 3D—OATMEAL 4D—HIDDEN
    **Bonus:** A singer, field, or rock—DIAMOND

13. **Answers:**
    1A—YANKEE 5A—LOTUS 6A—RINSE 7A—SLEEPY
    1D—YELLOW 2D—NATURAL 3D—ESSENCE 4D—MISERY
    **Bonus:** This person plays a doctor on TV—SEYMOUR

14. **Answers:**
    1A—NICOLE 5A—MABEL 6A—NEARS 7A—STAYED
    1D—NIMBUS 2D—CABINET 3D—LULLABY 4D—UNUSED
    **Bonus:** Length but not in inches or feet—DURATION

15. **Answers:**
    1A—RESUME 5A—LARGO 6A—ELLEN 7A—WHITER
    1D—RELIVE 2D—SCREECH 3D—MOONLIT 4D—TURNER
    **Bonus:** Enjoy—RELISH

16. **Answers:**
    1A—SCRIBE 5A—LAPEL 6A—ICING 7A—PEANUT
    1D—SPLINT 2D—REPTILE 3D—BILLION 4D—TARGET
    **Bonus:** Imagine—PICTURE

17. **Answers:**
    1A—GURGLE 5A—LILAC 6A—ADOBE 7A—SELECT
    1D—GALAXY 2D—RELEASE 3D—LACTOSE 4D—HONEST
    **Bonus:** The "H" in H. H., C. H., S. H., D. H., T. H., V. H., and R. H.—HUXTABLE

18. **Answers:**
    1A—ENTICE 5A—HOIST 6A— INANE 7A—FLAKES
    1D—EXHORT 2D—TRIVIAL 3D—CATWALK 4D—OBSESS
    **Bonus:** Spectator—ONLOOKER

19. **Answers:**
    1A—INSECT 5A—PAULA 6A—ELMER 7A—STORMY
    1D—IMPORT 2D—STUDENT 3D—CHARMER 4D—ENERGY
    **Bonus:** This often begins with a ceremony—MARRIAGE

20. **Answers:**
    1A—UNLOAD 5A—EDWIN 6A—UPSET 7A—OTTAWA
    1D—UNEVEN 2D—LAWSUIT 3D—AMNESIA 4D—AGATHA
    **Bonus:** A Harrison Ford movie—WITNESS

21. **Answers:**
    1A—COLLAR 5A—SLUMP 6A—DORIS 7A—TRASHY
    1D—CASHEW 2D—LAUNDER 3D—ASPIRES 4D—PIGSTY
    **Bonus:** You may be in yours now—HOMETOWN

22. **Answers:**
    1A—FLABBY 5A—TITLE 6A—CAKED 7A—NEURON
    1D—FATHER 2D—ARTICLE 3D—BREAKER 4D—JORDAN
    **Bonus:** Associated with "500"—DAYTONA

23. **Answers:**
    1A—STRIDE 5A—NICHE 6A—TEASE 7A—GLIDER
    1D—SANITY 2D—RECITAL 3D—DIEHARD 4D—CAREER
    **Bonus:** One of the famous "threesome"—CHRYSLER

24. **Answers:**
    1A—STRUCK 5A—LOGAN 6A—LOOSE 7A—PRETTY
    1D—SPLASH 2D—REGULAR 3D—CONSORT 4D—CHEERY
    **Bonus:** Sometimes marked with an "X"—TREASURE

25. **Answers:**
    1A—YOGURT 5A—LOUIS 6A—BLIMP 7A—HEDGES
    1D—YELLOW 2D—GRUMBLE 3D—RUSHING 4D—CAMPUS
    **Bonus:** This character's last name was "Lindstrom"—PHYLLIS

26. **Answers:**
    1A—BESIDE 5A—FORTE 6A—NOMAD 7A—GEORGE
    1D—BAFFLE 2D—STRANGE 3D—DREAMER 4D—WADDLE
    **Bonus:** Shoes—FOOTWEAR

27. **Answers:**
    1A—BOMBAY 5A—RUPEE 6A—EDITH 7A—ISLAND
    1D—BORDER 2D—MUPPETS 3D—AMERICA 4D—LASHED
    **Bonus:** Bread, milk, etc.—STAPLES

28. **Answers:**
    1A—FELLOW 5A—TENTH 6A—ELLEN 7A—ENRAGE
    1D—FATHOM 2D—LANTERN 3D—OPHELIA 4D—SPONGE
    **Bonus:** Very impressive—AWESOME

29. **Answers:**
    1A—TAHITI 5A—ADAGE 6A—HEAVE 7A—ARGYLL
    1D—TRAGIC 2D—HEATHER 3D—THERAPY 4D—ORWELL
    **Bonus:** This is usually cheaper—REPLICA

30. **Answers:**
    1A—WONDER 5A—AIMED 6A—RARER 7A—ELUDED
    1D—WEALTH 2D—NUMERAL 3D—ENDURED 4D—VEERED
    **Bonus:** Anytime—WHENEVER

31. **Answers:**
    1A—SHADOW 5A—NOTES 6A—AGREE 7A—DETECT
    1D—SENIOR 2D—ACTUATE 3D—OBSERVE 4D—EFFECT
    **Bonus:** You can get caught *in* this—BETWEEN

32. **Answers:**
    1A—LAVISH 5A—TUBER 6A—ARISE 7A—STREWN
    1D—LETHAL 2D—VIBRANT 3D—SURVIVE 4D—INTERN
    **Bonus:** This *Bill* played a popular "Jim"—SHATNER

33. **Answers:**
    1A—MARTHA 5A—TWIST 6A—SMELT 7A—DENTED
    1D—MOTIVE 2D—REISSUE 3D—HOTTEST 4D—LISTED
    **Bonus:** Sometimes used like *easier*—DOWNHILL

34. **Answers:**
    1A—CARPET 5A—TUNIS 6A—INEPT 7A—AGENCY
    1D—CITRUS 2D—RUNNING 3D—EASTERN 4D—POETRY
    **Bonus:** Some say this can't be *stopped*—PROGRESS

35. **Answers:**
    1A—JUMBLE 5A—RANDY 6A—TALON 7A—CRAYON
    1D—JERSEY 2D—MONITOR 3D—LOYALTY 4D—CANNON
    **Bonus:** *In* and *out*—ANTONYMS

36. **Answers:**
    1A—FAMILY 5A—NIXON 6A—ENACT 7A—OLDEST
    1D—FENDER 2D—MAXWELL 3D—LINEAGE 4D—SEPTET
    **Bonus:** Sometimes done in *grand* fashion—OPENING

37. **Answers:**
1A—NOTICE 5A—PANDA 6A—EXTRA 7A—STARVE
1D—NAPLES 2D—TANGENT 3D—CHATTER 4D—FACADE
**Bonus:** This takes up approximately 210, 000 square miles—
FRANCE

38. **Answers:**
1A—POLAND 5A—GIRLS 6A—CELLO 7A—CLASSY
1D—PAGODA 2D—LYRICAL 3D—NESTLES 4D—CANOPY
**Bonus:** After Buchanan, before Johnson—LINCOLN

39. **Answers:**
1A—TOMATO 5A—CONGA 6A—OILED 7A—ENTREE
1D—TUCKER 2D—MONSOON 3D—TRAILER 4D—SUNDAE
**Bonus:** This can be *graded*—GASOLINE

40. **Answers:**
1A—DIVOTS 5A—SONIC 6A—LIEGE 7A—BALSAM
1D—DASHED 2D—VANILLA 3D—TICKETS 4D—REDEEM
**Bonus:** *Quickly, suddenly,* and *hurriedly*—ADVERBS

41. **Answers:**
1A—FOSTER 5A—LIONS 6A—ALLEN 7A—LEADEN
1D—FILTER 2D—STORAGE 3D—ENSILED 4D—PENNON
**Bonus:** A reason to keep going—INERTIA

42. **Answers:**
1A—GALLON 5A—ROBIN 6A—TABLE 7A—FRESCO
1D—GARLIC 2D—LOBSTER 3D—OMNIBUS 4D—GAZEBO
**Bonus:** Unknown—FOREIGN

43. **Answers:**
1A—TRUMAN 5A—IRENE 6A—ULTRA 7A—ELUDES
1D—THIRST 2D—UNEQUAL 3D—AVERTED 4D—PETALS
**Bonus:** *Hot* _____—PURSUIT

44. **Answers:**
1A—MISTER 5A—LEASE 6A—PRESS 7A—FOSTER
1D—MILLET 2D—SHAMPOO 3D—ELEMENT 4D—CENSOR
**Bonus:** After *picture* and before *score*—PERFECT

45. **Answers:**
1A—TRANCE 5A—TACKS 6A—ELITE 7A—ATONED
1D—TATTOO 2D—ANCIENT 3D—CUSHION 4D—DEPEND
**Bonus:** Etiquette—PROTOCOL

46. **Answers:**
1A—PARODY 5A—ROBIN 6A—CLEAR 7A—BANNER
1D—PIRATE 2D—REBECCA 3D—DUNGEON 4D—NEARER
**Bonus:** You don't have to have paper to *draw* one—CURTAIN

47. **Answers:**
1A—BUCKLE 5A—SCRAM 6A—AHEAD 7A—GLUTEN
1D—BISHOP 2D—CURTAIL 3D—LAMBENT 4D—CORDON
**Bonus:** Show—INDICATE

48. **Answers:**
1A—FUTILE 5A—GUESS 6A—ERICA 7A—GAUGED
1D—FIGURE 2D—THERESA 3D—LASTING 4D—HOWARD
**Bonus:** "8"—AUGUST

49. **Answers:**
1A—DREAMS 5A—VITAL 6A—AGNES 7A—ENDEAR
1D—DEVISE 2D—ENTRAIN 3D—MELANIE 4D—CAESAR
**Bonus:** Remedy—MEDICINE

50. **Answers:**
1A—RUPERT 5A—LINDA 6A—CATER 7A—DEARTH
1D—RELICS 2D—PANACHE 3D—ROASTER 4D—STARCH
**Bonus:** Kelly, Rogers, etc.—DANCERS

51. **Answers:**
1A—DEPICT 5A—OMEGA 6A—INTRA 7A—GEORGE
1D—DROWSY 2D—PREMISE 3D—CHAPTER 4D—MENACE
**Bonus:** You are one of these—READERS

52. **Answers:**
1A—FIRMLY 5A—RESET 6A—DARTS 7A—REPLAY
1D—FERRET 2D—RESIDUE 3D—LATERAL 4D—DRESSY
**Bonus:** "Over," in *over* and *over*—REPEATED

53. **Answers:**
1A—HARPER 5A—BOTCH 6A—NINTH 7A—PATENT
1D—HUBBLE 2D—ROTUNDA 3D—ENHANCE 4D—UPSHOT
**Bonus:** Hamilton, Wellington, and Sofia—CAPITALS

54. **Answers:**
1A—GORDON 5A—NASTY 6A—REPEL 7A—HERALD
1D—GINGER 2D—RESERVE 3D—OLYMPIA 4D—BALLAD
**Bonus:** Usually bigger and bolder, easy to spot—HEADLINE

55. **Answers:**
1A—THAMES 5A—GRACE 6A—NOISE 7A—STAGES
1D—TAGGED 2D—AGAINST 3D—EVENING 4D—ATHENS
**Bonus:** Together—INTACT

56. **Answers:**
1A—CHANCE 5A—SLIDE 6A—ANKLE 7A—TENDER
1D—CUSTOM 2D—ANIMATE 3D—CHECKED 4D—APPEAR
**Bonus:** One way you will never see these puzzles—UNEDITED

57. **Answers:**
1A—RUSTLE 5A—CARGO 6A—TRIED 7A—SHAGGY
1D—RECALL 2D—STRETCH 3D—LOOMING 4D—DEADLY
**Bonus:** It takes time for you to reach this—ADULTHOOD

58. **Answers:**
1A—RIDDLE 5A—SECTS 6A—ALIEN 7A—LENGTH
1D—RESIDE 2D—DECLARE 3D—LASTING 4D—FLINCH
**Bonus:** Begin—INITIATE

59. **Answers:**
1A—PUNDIT 5A—DICEY 6A—SOLAR 7A—MADCAP
1D—PEDALS 2D—NICOSIA 3D—IDYLLIC 4D—ENTRAP
**Bonus:** This can bring about a significant change—CATALYST

60. **Answers:**
1A—MUSTER 5A—RELIC 6A—CUPID 7A—UNLESS
1D—MURMUR 2D—SILICON 3D—ESCAPEE 4D—EXODUS
**Bonus:** Problem—DILEMMA

61. **Answers:**
1A—CANADA 5A—BLUES 6A—RAPID 7A—FLANGE
1D—COBALT 2D—NEUTRAL 3D—DUSTPAN 4D—DAWDLE
**Bonus:** Clue: Repeat Clue: Repeat—DUPLICATE

62. **Answers:**
1A—VANITY 5A—RIPEN 6A—UNION 7A—KENNEL
1D—VIRTUE 2D—NEPTUNE 3D—TENSION 4D—TUNNEL
**Bonus:** Three on this side and four on that side—UNEVEN

63. **Answers:**
1A—TROWEL 5A—BATES 6A—ABATE 7A—CELERY
1D—TABLES 2D—OUTRAGE 3D—ENSNARE 4D—SOLELY
**Bonus:** Yours can be *raised*—EYEBROWS

64. **Answers:**
1A—DISARM 5A—SHELF 6A—ITALY 7A—SLATED
1D—DISOWN 2D—SPECIAL 3D—REFRACT 4D—OBEYED
**Bonus:** "He" is one, but "She" is not—ELEMENT (HELIUM)

65. **Answers:**
1A—KANSAS 5A—TOWER 6A—OUNCE 7A—STEERS
1D—KITTEN 2D—NEWPORT 3D—ARRANGE 4D—BICEPS
**Bonus:** "Jonas Grumby"—THE SKIPPER

66. **Answers:**
1A—ANGOLA 5A—BLAST 6A—MURAL 7A—FRILLS
1D—ALBERT 2D—GRAMMAR 3D—LITERAL 4D—SPILLS
**Bonus:** 1+1+? and a broken radiator—PROBLEMS

67. **Answers:**
1A—AGREED 5A—TEPEE 6A—ABNER 7A—MERLIN
1D—ACTION 2D—REPLACE 3D—ETERNAL 4D—PATRON
**Bonus:** It doesn't cost you anything to *pay* this—ATTENTION

68. **Answers:**
1A—FIGURE 5A—CLANG 6A—UNTIE 7A—ALWAYS
1D—FACIAL 2D—GRADUAL 3D—REGATTA 4D—POWERS
**Bonus:** Yours is yet to be determined—LIFE SPAN

69. **Answers:**
1A—GREASE 5A—DRAMA 6A—UTTER 7A—SECRET
1D—GADGET 2D—ERASURE 3D—SPATTER 4D—CARROT
**Bonus:** You can watch one kind or hold another—PROGRAM

70. **Answers:**
1A—ADVICE 5A—FORUM 6A—IDEAL 7A—STATUS
1D—AFFIRM 2D—VERDICT 3D—COMMENT 4D—DALLAS
**Bonus:** "I would love to hear from you ____ _____"—
VIA E-MAIL

71. **Answers:**
1A—DEDUCT 5A—INFER 6A—OUNCE 7A—STORED
1D—DAINTY 2D—DEFROST 3D—CORONER 4D—EXCEED
**Bonus:** Although not a "white meat," this does have white
meat—COCONUT

72. **Answers:**
1A—FATHER 5A—LEASE  6A—PANTS 7A—DEGREE
1D—FELONY 2D—TRAMPLE 3D—ELEANOR 4D—PURSUE
**Bonus:** A North American city—MONTREAL

73. **Answers:**
1A—AUTUMN 5A—STALL 6A—PROWL 7A—CRUMMY
1D—ASSUME 2D—TRAPPER 3D—MALCOLM 4D—PULLEY
**Bonus:** Man and a manatee—MAMMALS

74. **Answers:**
1A—CLOVER 5A—MUCUS 6A—ARENA  7A—ADONIS
1D—COMMON 2D—ORCHARD 3D—EASTERN 4D—HARASS
**Bonus:** This can be a weight or a person—ANCHOR

185

75. **Answers:**
1A—TURKEY 5A—PLATO 6A—TWICE 7A—BRUNCH
1D—TYPIFY 2D—ROASTER 3D—EMOTION 4D—JOSEPH
**Bonus:** Christopher Jones was its captain—MAYFLOWER

76. **Answers:**
1A—ABSENT 5A—BONUS 6A—TYLER 7A—CRADLE
1D—AUBURN 2D—SENATOR 3D—NESTLED 4D—SOURCE
**Bonus:** (                    )—CLUELESS

77. **Answers:**
1A—POETRY 5A—LYING 6A—OCTET 7A—MENACE
1D—PALMER 2D—EPISODE 3D—REGATTA 4D—BUSTLE
**Bonus:** These can pass or be written down—MINUTES

78. **Answers:**
1A—SEARCH 5A—AMBER 6A—NOISE 7A—PARCEL
1D—STATUE 2D—ALBANIA 3D—CARDIAC 4D—APPEAL
**Bonus:** A broad classification—REPTILE

79. **Answers:**
1A—SALAMI 5A—SIREN 6A—LIENS 7A—DIESEL
1D—SESAME 2D—LORELEI 3D—MONKEES 4D—TASSEL
**Bonus:** D.J., M.N., P.T., and M.D.—INITIALS

80. **Answers:**
1A—FORMAL 5A—RESET 6A—INNER 7A—ARMADA
1D—FARMER 2D—RISKIER 3D—ANTENNA 4D—SIERRA
**Bonus:** Three of this show's four stars have first names that start with "J"—SEINFELD

81. **Answers:**
1A—SUPERB 5A—OWNED 6A—OSCAR 7A—WALLET
1D—SHOVEL 2D—PANDORA 3D—RADICAL 4D—PARROT
**Bonus:** Total, end to end—OVERALL

82. **Answers:**
1A—ANSWER 5A—ENDED 6A—EARTH 7A—ASCEND
1D—AVENGE 2D—SADNESS 3D—ENDORSE 4D—LASHED
**Bonus:** Did not go together—CLASHED

83. **Answers:**
1A—KANSAS 5A—DIMES 6A—NINTH 7A—HEALED
1D—KIDDIE 2D—NOMINEE 3D—ARSENAL 4D—MASHED
**Bonus:** *One of my biggest fears*—MISTAKES

84. **Answers:**
1A—SORROW 5A—NIMOY 6A—APPLE 7A—TEACUP
1D—SANDAL 2D—RAMPAGE 3D—OLYMPIC 4D—ASLEEP
**Bonus:** This is sometimes *given*—ASYLUM

85. **Answers:**
1A—MODIFY 5A—TONGS 6A—IDEAL 7A—STATIC
1D—METHOD 2D—DENTIST 3D—FASTEST 4D—GARLIC
**Bonus:** A famous performer—SINATRA

86. **Answers:**
1A—PUZZLE 5A—NASTY 6A—FILER 7A—SLAYED
1D—PENCIL 2D—ZESTFUL 3D—LOYALTY 4D—SACRED
**Bonus:** *Natural*—DISASTERS

87. **Answers:**
1A—LAURIE 5A—PERIL 6A—VOCAL 7A—PLATED
1D—LOPPED 2D—UNRAVEL 3D—ILLICIT 4D—MAILED
**Bonus:** Longer play or higher pay—OVERTIME

88. **Answers:**
1A—CREDIT 5A—CUBES 6A—SLATE 7A—SYSTEM
1D—CUCKOO 2D—EMBASSY 3D—INSTANT 4D—MUSEUM
**Bonus:** "This" is it—BONUS CLUE

89. **Answers:**
1A—HOMAGE 5A—KAREN 6A—COSMO 7A—LESSON
1D—HIKING 2D—MIRACLE 3D—GENESIS 4D—UPTOWN
**Bonus:** Important—SPECIAL

90. **Answers:**
1A—AVENUE 5A—LACES 6A—ORATE 7A—SENTRY
1D—AILING 2D—ENCLOSE 3D—UPSTART 4D—NINETY
**Bonus:** No—NEGATIVE

91. **Answers:**
1A—GATHER 5A—SHRUG 6A—IMAGE 7A—CEMENT
1D—GOSSIP 2D—TERMITE 3D—ENGRAVE 4D—UNREST
**Bonus:** *David L. Hoyt*—SIGNATURE

92. **Answers:**
1A—POSTER 5A—DRONE 6A—MANGO 7A—ANKLET
1D—PODIUM 2D—SNOWMAN 3D—ETERNAL 4D—EFFORT
**Bonus:** *Fast*—FORWARD

93. **Answers:**
1A—NAPLES 5A—LINGO 6A—AMINO 7A—BLENDS
1D—NELSON 2D—PINBALL 3D—EROSION 4D—NYLONS
**Bonus:** A type of basketball game or conversation—ONE ON ONE

94. **Answers:**
1A—THEORY 5A—SCUFF 6A—INANE 7A—SEANCE
1D—TOSSED 2D—ELUSIVE 3D—REFRAIN 4D—AMPERE
**Bonus:** RADAR and MASH—ACRONYMS

95. **Answers:**
1A—EULOGY 5A—TIGER 6A—OFFER 7A—INDEED
1D—ENTITY 2D—LEGHORN 3D—GIRAFFE 4D—CONRAD
**Bonus:** One type has four legs, another has four wheels—GREYHOUND

96. **Answers:**
1A—NEWARK 5A—CHRIS 6A—ALONE 7A—OTHERS
1D—NICOLE 2D—WARRANT 3D—RESTORE 4D—POWERS
**Bonus:** *I would give you mine, if you asked for it*—OPINION

97. **Answers:**
1A—DEMAND 5A—POINT 6A—TORCH 7A—ANTLER
1D—DEPEND 2D—MOISTEN 3D—NATURAL 4D—GOPHER
**Bonus:** You must be male to be one—GRANDSON

98. **Answers:**
1A—LENGTH 5A—TAMPA 6A—RANGE 7A—OLDEST
1D—LOTION 2D—NUMERAL 3D—TRAINEE 4D—DIGEST
**Bonus:** Busy—ON THE GO

99. **Answers:**
1A—UNWRAP 5A—STAIR 6A—HENCE 7A—PROMPT
1D—UNSAID 2D—WEATHER 3D—ACRONYM 4D—SILENT
**Bonus:** *My wish to you . . . Happy _____.*—HOLIDAYS

100. **Answers:**
1A—PELLET 5A—PANIC 6A—AWASH 7A—DELETE
1D—PUPILS 2D—LINEAGE 3D—ENCLAVE 4D—ARCHIE
**Bonus:** Sustained, severe decline—TAILSPIN

101. **Answers:**
1A—FORBID 5A—MOVIE 6A—ROAST 7A—FENDER
1D—FAMOUS 2D—REVERSE 3D—ICELAND 4D—CRATER
**Bonus:** A type of conversation you can't have on the telephone—FACE TO FACE

102. **Answers:**
1A—THRIVE 5A—INCUR 6A—TWIRL 7A—FLINCH
1D—TRICKY 2D—RECITAL 3D—VERSION 4D—HEALTH
**Bonus:** Their location may determine their price—TICKETS

103. **Answers:**
1A—GREASE 5A—BEETS 6A—ISAAC 7A—AGENDA
1D—GOBLET 2D—EVENING 3D—SUSTAIN 4D—MARCIA
**Bonus:** Found at the bottom of the sea—TITANIC

104. **Answers:**
1A—ODDITY 5A—THORN 6A—PLATO 7A—URGENT
1D—OUTFIT 2D—DROPPER 3D—TONNAGE 4D—SPROUT
**Bonus:** A type of output—PRINTOUT

105. **Answers:**
1A—SLIGHT 5A—RIDES 6A—LYING 7A—HEREBY
1D—SCRIMP 2D—INDULGE 3D—HOSTILE 4D—TWIGGY
**Bonus:** A land connector—ISTHMUS

106. **Answers:**
1A—PLEDGE 5A—PETER 6A—EDICT 7A—TETHER
1D—POPLAR 2D—EXTREME 3D—GARNISH 4D—PEWTER
**Bonus:** *Chicken* is one variety of this—POTPIE

107. **Answers:**
1A—OTTAWA 5A—REGAL 6A—TROLL 7A—CREEPY
1D—ONRUSH 2D—TIGHTER 3D—WELCOME 4D—REALLY
**Bonus:** This is home to approximately 10 million people—PORTUGAL

108. **Answers:**
1A—STAPLE 5A—IDAHO 6A—INEPT 7A—UNISON
1D—SPICED 2D—ARABIAN 3D—LIONESS 4D—CARTON
**Bonus:** *I need these . . . You may or may not*—CONTACTS

109. **Answers:**
1A—DECODE 5A—RELIC 6A—EMBER 7A—ITALIC
1D—DURESS 2D—COLLECT 3D—DECIBEL 4D—NITRIC
**Bonus:** Event—OCCURRENCE

110. **Answers:**
1A—BRUTUS 5A—LUCID 6A—VERSE 7A—TROOPS
1D—BALLAD 2D—UNCOVER 3D—UNDERGO 4D—WIPERS
**Bonus:** *I had _____ _____ for breakfast today*—TWO BAGELS

111. **Answers:**
1A—ALUMNI 5A—BREAM 6A—RANGE 7A—CHALET
1D—ALBANY 2D—UNEARTH 3D—NOMINAL 4D—EXTENT
**Bonus:** *If someone can solve this whole puzzle in under 60 seconds, and email me to tell me about it at DLHoyt@aol.com, I will donate some money to a good cause.*—CHALLENGE

112. **Answers:**
1A—PLACID 5A—SHAWN 6A—NOTES 7A—STUDIO
1D—PESTER 2D—AGAINST 3D—IGNITED 4D—FIASCO
**Bonus:** Valid—AUTHENTIC

113. **Answers:**
1A—ENGULF 5A—VELUM 6A—LAIRS 7A—BOGGLE
1D—ENVIED 2D—GALILEO 3D—LEMMING 4D—LASSIE
**Bonus:** *Im & frnd* —ILLEGIBLE

114. **Answers:**
1A—JIGSAW 5A—STUFF 6A—BOXES 7A—VENDOR
1D—JOSEPH 2D—GRUMBLE 3D—AFFIXED 4D—CAESAR
**Bonus:** Place together—JUXTAPOSE

115. **Answers:**
1A—JIGSAW 5A—STUFF 6A—BOXES 7A—VENDOR
1D—JOSEPH 2D—GRUMBLE 3D—AFFIXED 4D—CAESAR
**Bonus:** You can feel this, but you can't touch it—DEJA VU

116. **Answers:**
1A—RODENT 5A—TOTEM 6A—ORDER 7A—STACKS
1D—ROTUND 2D—DETROIT 3D—NOMADIC 4D—DEBRIS
**Bonus:** ██████ —SMEARED

117. **Answers:**
1A—GLADLY 5A—OFTEN 6A—REMIT 7A—ADONIS
1D—GROCER 2D—ATTIRED 3D—LINEMAN 4D—GRATIS
**Bonus:** Archibald Leach's stage name—CARY GRANT

118. **Answers:**
1A—LARIAT 5A—DOING 6A—BREAD 7A—SWATHE
1D—LODGES 2D—RAINBOW 3D—AUGMENT 4D—NOODLE
**Bonus:** *I was _____ when I made this puzzle*—OUTDOORS

119. **Answers:**
1A—SPRAWL 5A—TEMPO 6A—NEPAL 7A—FERRET
1D—SATURN 2D—ROMANCE 3D—WHOPPER 4D—HAMLET
**Bonus:** This was patented on January 30, 1885—ROLLER
COASTER

120. **Answers:**
1A—ACROSS 5A—TEASE 6A—TIRED 7A—TRADED
1D—ANTHEM 2D—REACTOR 3D—SHEARED 4D—LANDED
**Bonus:** A reason to turn around—DEAD END

121. **Answers:**
1A—DURESS 5A—LATHE 6A—LILAC 7A—TRACED
1D—DOLLAR 2D—RATTLER 3D—SHELLAC 4D—MINCED
**Bonus:** Position—SITUATION

122. **Answers:**
1A— OFFEND 5A—JANET 6A—INLET 7A—AGREED
1D—OBJECT 2D—FENCING 3D—NATALIE 4D—VESTED
**Bonus:** Drop—NOSEDIVE

123. **Answers:**
1A—WEASEL 5A—MOTEL 6A—CAPER 7A—VENEER
1D—WOMBAT 2D—ARTICLE 3D—ELLIPSE 4D—HORROR
**Bonus:** "The next bonus will reference this bonus," for example—
PREVIEW

124. **Answers:**
1A—STOKER 5A—HYENA 6A—ALTER 7A—FENDER
1D—SCHOOL 2D—OPERATE 3D—ENACTED 4D—BEARER
**Bonus:** The previous bonus answer was "preview"—
FLASHBACK

125. **Answers:**
1A—REFUGE 5A—MINCE 6A—RULER 7A—PLENTY
1D—REMOTE 2D—FUNERAL 3D—GREMLIN 4D—HEARTY
**Bonus:** Again and again—TIME AFTER TIME

126. **Answers:**
1A—MUSTER 5A—CLASP 6A—TOWED 7A—HEARSE
1D—MOCKED 2D—SEATTLE 3D—EMPOWER 4D—FIDDLE
**Bonus:** John Wayne's father's profession—PHARMACIST

127. **Answers:**
1A—BUDGET 5A—PANEL 6A—INPUT 7A—STREET
1D—BOPPED 2D—DENTIST 3D—ECLIPSE 4D—SEPTET
**Bonus:** Crazy—LUDICROUS

128. **Answers:**
1A—OCCUPY 5A—PIPER 6A—ELUDE 7A—ISOBAR
1D—OPPOSE 2D—CYPRESS 3D—PERTURB 4D—METEOR
**Bonus:** Now and then—SPORADIC

129. **Answers:**
1A—RATIFY 5A—SEOUL 6A—PEACE 7A—GRIEVE
1D—RUSTLE 2D—TROOPER 3D—FOLIAGE 4D—SECEDE
**Bonus:** Mean—SPITEFUL

130. **Answers:**
1A—MUPPET 5A—TROOP 6A—ACUTE 7A—JEREMY
1D—MOTIVE 2D—PROBATE 3D—ESPOUSE 4D—REMEDY
**Bonus:** Edge—PERIMETER

131. **Answers:**
1A—GULPED 5A—TAXED 6A—CURED 7A—UNISON
1D—GATHER 2D—LEXICON 3D—ENDURES 4D—MAIDEN
**Bonus:** Difficult—ARDUOUS

132. **Answers:**
1A—TOPPLE 5A—CLINT 6A—BRUCE 7A—REVEAL
1D—TICKLE 2D—PLIABLE 3D—LETTUCE 4D—ORDEAL
**Bonus:** Enjoyable—DELECTABLE

133. **Answers:**
1A—PALMER 5A—MANOR 6A—EXTRA 7A—STICKY
1D— PUMPED 2D—LONGEST 3D—ERRATIC 4D—INFAMY
**Bonus:** *I made several of these the other day . . . I enjoyed
every one of them*—PUTTS FOR PAR

134. **Answers:**
1A—MICKEY 5A—FROST 6A—PEARL 7A—ARTIC
1D—MUFFIN 2D—CHOPPER 3D—EXTRACT 4D—PUBLIC
**Bonus:** Groupings—FAMILIES

135. **Answers:**
1A—CARAFE 5A—MODEL 6A—ABIDE 7A—BENGAL
1D—COMMON 2D—RADIATE 3D—FILLING 4D—UNVEIL
**Bonus:** Shape—CONDITION

136. **Answers:**
1A—NOTICED 5A—RECUR 6A—FEUDS 7A—SOLVENT
1D—NERVOUS 2D—TACTFUL 3D—CAROUSE 4D—DEPOSIT
**Bonus:** Different—UNUSUAL

137. **Answers:**
1A—CORTEZ 5A—GAMES 6A—NYLON 7A—LEANED
1D—COGNAC 2D—ROMANCE 3D—EPSILON 4D—DAWNED
**Bonus:** This character goes by "Gojira" in Japan—GODZILLA

138. **Answers:**
1A—HELIUM 5A—CATER 6A—ROGER 7A—PLATES
1D—HECTIC 2D—LATERAL 3D—UPRIGHT 4D—CHORUS
**Bonus:** Maybe—PERHAPS

139. **Answers:**
1A—CHROME 5A—FELON 6A—PLATO 7A—FEMALE
1D—COFFIN 2D—RELAPSE 3D—MONTANA 4D—EUROPE
**Bonus:** This is something you can see on a regular basis, but
not every day—FULL MOON

140. **Answers:**
1A—SHELVE 5A—FARCE 6A—ERNIE 7A—STYMIE
1D—SAFARI 2D—EARNEST 3D—VIETNAM 4D—SLEEVE
**Bonus:** The longest of its kind—NILE RIVER

141. **Answers:**
1A—GALLON 5A—AWFUL 6A—INGOT 7A—FRIDAY
1D—GRADED 2D—LOFTIER 3D—OBLIGED 4D—SENTRY
**Bonus:** This creature has existed on Earth for over 250 million
years—DRAGONFLY

142. **Answers:**
1A—ELAPSE 5A—CRIMP 6A—AROMA 7A—MENTOR
1D—EXCESS 2D—AGITATE 3D—SUPPORT 4D—IMPAIR
**Bonus:** Home to approximately 4 million—LOUISIANA

143. **Answers:**
1A—AGENDA 5A—CAROL 6A—HOVER 7A—STURDY
1D—ARCHIE 2D—EARSHOT 3D—DELIVER 4D—DEARLY
**Bonus:** Conversation—DIALOGUE

144. **Answers:**
1A—ISOBAR 5A—EXTRA 6A—MAINE 7A—AMENDS
1D—ICEMAN 2D—OPTIMUM 3D—ARABIAN 4D—PANELS
**Bonus:** *I have no chance of experiencing this*—LABOR PAIN

145. **Answers:**
1A—ROTATE 5A—BEING 6A—KITES 7A—STONES
1D—ROBERT 2D—THICKET 3D—TIGHTEN 4D—CRISIS
**Bonus:** Having the clues upside down, for example—
IRRITATING

146. **Answers:**
1A—DIVERT 5A—SCRAM 6A—OSAKA 7A—GENTLE
1D—DISMAY 2D—VERBOSE 3D—RAMPANT 4D—HOMAGE
**Bonus:** *I am one*—OMNIVORE

147. **Answers:**
1A—ACCEPT 5A—ISSUE 6A—IDIOT 7A—INDEED
1D—APIECE 2D—CASPIAN 3D—PREMISE 4D—SLATED
**Bonus:** Great—SPLENDID

148. **Answers:**
1A—MOTHER 5A—NAMES 6A—EMEND 7A—STONES
1D—MANGOS 2D—TEMPEST 3D—EASTERN 4D—EXODUS
**Bonus:** *I am not one but you might be*—DAUGHTER

149. **Answers:**
1A—SCULPT 5A—SCRAM 6A—VINYL 7A—ALMOND
1D—SESAME 2D—UNRAVEL 3D—PIMENTO 4D—EYELID
**Bonus:** *I've never had one*—MANICURE

150. **Answers:**
1A—ENSURE 5A—TOUGH 6A—TERSE 7A—ARISES
1D—ENTAIL 2D—SAUNTER 3D—REHIRES 4D—UTTERS
**Bonus:** Circular 15th—THE LETTER "O"

151. **Answers:**
1A—TENURE 5A—SCRAP 6A—ALTER 7A—VENDOR
1D—TESTED 2D—NARRATE 3D—REPUTED 4D—MIRROR
**Bonus:** Move—MANEUVER

152. **Answers:**
1A—PIGLET 5A—SOLVE 6A—LEDGE 7A—WONDER
1D—PISTON 2D—GALILEO 3D—EMENDED 4D—APPEAR
**Bonus:** *I was born in ___ _____*—NEW ENGLAND

153. **Answers:**
1A—SICILY 5A—AGLOW 6A—REEVE 7A—STASIS
1D—SHANTY 2D—CULPRIT 3D—LAWLESS 4D—NOVELS
**Bonus:** Sometimes used like "departed"—ON YOUR WAY

154. **Answers:**
1A—TAHITI 5A—LUCID 6A—LEERS 7A—GRITTY
1D—TOLLED 2D—HECKLER 3D—TIDIEST 4D—MEASLY
**Bonus:** Home to approximately 3 million people—ROME, ITALY

155. **Answers:**
1A—JOCKEY 5A—MOIST 6A—GRASP 7A—LETTER
1D—JUMBLE 2D—CRINGLE 3D—ENTRANT 4D—HAMPER
**Bonus:** 4, 5, 6—APRIL, MAY, JUNE

156. **Answers:**
1A—BECKON 5A—HAITI 6A—ARISE 7A—BOUNTY
1D—BEHOLD 2D—CHICAGO 3D—OPINION 4D—TIMELY
**Bonus:** Home to approximately one million people—MANITOBA

157. **Answers:**
1A—NECTAR 5A—CIRCA 6A—AISLE 7A—ELUDES
1D—NICOLE 2D—CURTAIL 3D—AMASSED 4D—FLEETS
**Bonus:** This person died in 479 B.C.—CONFUCIUS

158. **Answers:**
1A—CATTLE 5A—BRAVO 6A—PIANO 7A—NEEDLE
1D—COBWEB 2D—TRAIPSE 3D—LEOTARD 4D—REVOKE
**Bonus:** Reserve—STOCKPILE

159. **Answers:**
1A—UPHELD 5A—CARGO 6A—INERT 7A—STAYED
1D—UNCORK 2D—HARPIST 3D—LOOSELY 4D—MELTED
**Bonus:** Food—NOURISHMENT

160. **Answers:**
1A—WREATH 5A—RULER 6A—POUND 7A—NEPHEW
1D—WARMTH 2D—ECLIPSE 3D—THROUGH 4D—SHADOW
**Bonus:** *I am one . . . You may or may not be*—GROWNUP

161. **Answers:**
1A—PLUNGE 5A—TIARA 6A—INDIA 7A—IMPART
1D—PETITE 2D—URANIUM 3D—GRANDMA 4D—THWART
**Bonus:** _____ __ ___ new year—RING IN THE

162. **Answers:**
1A—SAIGON 5A—MOVIE 6A—DRAIN 7A—GRILLS
1D—SYMBOL 2D—INVADER 3D—OVERALL 4D—TAINTS
**Bonus:** January 1, for example—BEGINNING

163. **Answers:**
1A—GOTTEN 5A—SMASH 6A—TINGE 7A—GRILLS
1D—GASHED 2D—TOASTER 3D—ETHANOL 4D—TOKENS
**Bonus:** Honest—STRAIGHT

164. **Answers:**
1A—GYRATE 5A—ROSIE 6A—ORBIT 7A—LEGEND
1D—GIRDER 2D—RISSOLE 3D—TREMBLE 4D—SLATED
**Bonus:** Intentional—BY DESIGN

165. **Answers:**
1A—GEMINI 5A—LAGER 6A—CLONE 7A—CLOSET
1D—GOLDEN 2D—MAGICAL 3D—NERVOUS 4D—HONEST
**Double Bonus:** Covered—SHINGLED
Found on a quadruped—HIND LEGS

166. **Answers:**
1A—SPRING 5A—RIFLE 6A—AWFUL 7A—ANTLER
1D—SHRUNK 2D—REFRAIN 3D—NEEDFUL 4D—TAILOR
**Double Bonus:** Under another circumstance—OTHERWISE
Floral gift—WHITE ROSE

167. **Answers:**
1A—EARWIG 5A—CUBIT 6A—INURE 7A—CHEERS
1D—EXCISE 2D—RUBBISH 3D—INTRUDE 4D—FACETS
**Bonus:** Gift—FREEBIE
Sturdier—BEEFIER

168. **Answers:**
1A—INDIGO 5A—PASSE 6A—UNTIL 7A—STURDY
1D—IMPART 2D—DISGUST 3D—GREATER 4D—DEPLOY
**Double Bonus:** Someone to root for—UNDERDOG
Based—GROUNDED

169. **Answers:**
1A—REGALE 5A—ALIGN 6A—ALIEN 7A—BEAGLE
1D—REASON 2D—GRIMACE 3D—LONGING 4D—TWINGE
**Double Bonus:** Frightening—ALARMING
Not of the central importance—MARGINAL

170. **Answers:**
1A—DILUTE 5A—SEVEN 6A—BLOOD 7A—MEDLEY
1D—DESIRE 2D—LOVABLE 3D—TINFOIL 4D—HEYDAY
**Double Bonus:** A reason to stop—FINISHED
Sinister—FIENDISH

171. **Answers:**
1A—ENDING 5A—CAPER 6A—EDICT 7A—PEGGED
1D—ENCASE 2D—DEPLETE 3D—NURSING 4D—TOUTED
**Double Bonus:** Exploded—ERUPTED
Supposed—REPUTED

172. **Answers:**
1A—ISOPOD 5A—CRISP 6A—TREES 7A—EDISON
1D—INCHES 2D—OMITTED 3D—OPPRESS 4D—PARSON
**Double Bonus:** Boats—CANOES
Waters—OCEANS

173. **Answers:**
1A—RAMROD 5A—HENCE 6A—ALLOT 7A—SAMPLE
1D—REHASH 2D—MONTANA 3D—OVERLAP 4D—TIPTOE
**Double Bonus:** Stupid—MORONIC
A Greek letter—OMICRON

174. **Answers:**
1A—NASSAU 5A—CREDO 6A—ABACK 7A—RENOWN
1D—NICKED 2D—SEEPAGE 3D—AVOCADO 4D—SICKEN
**Double Bonus:** Position—BEARINGS
Intrudes—BARGES IN

175. **Answers:**
1A—DANGLE 5A—MERIT 6A—USHER 7A—MENDED
1D—DAMAGE 2D—NUTURE 3D—LATCHED 4D—TORRID
**Double Bonus:** Reduced—TRIMMED
A halfway point—MID-TERM

176. **Answers:**
1A—SPRUCE 5A—CATHY 6A—HOTEL 7A—STUCCO
1D—SOCIAL 2D—RATCHET 3D—CRYPTIC 4D—APOLLO
**Double Bonus:** Roughest—HARSHEST
Whips—THRASHES

177. **Answers:**
1A—GOPHER 5A—NICHE 6A—FATAL 7A—SCORCH
1D—GENTRY 2D—PACIFIC 3D—ERECTOR 4D—WEALTH
**Double Bonus:** Building material—SHINGLE
Deliberate spin—ENGLISH

178. **Answers:**
1A—NUDGED 5A—CAVES 6A—LUNAR 7A—LEGEND
1D—NECTAR 2D—DIVULGE 3D—ESSENCE 4D—STORED
**Double Bonus:** Provoked—TAUNTED
Made aware—ATTUNED

179. **Answers:**
1A—TANGLE 5A—PARIS 6A—ALIAS 7A—MERGER
1D—TOPPED 2D—NARRATE 3D—LASTING 4D—PURSER
**Double Bonus:** Move—MIGRATE
_____ music—RAGTIME

180. **Answers:**
1A—RITUAL 5A—OMAHA 6A—PADRE 7A—HERNIA
1D—ROOSTS 2D—TRAIPSE 3D—ABANDON 4D—CINEMA
**Double Bonus:** _____ plane—SUPERSONIC
_____ instrument—PERCUSSION